YOU C
SPEAK SPANISH!

A STEP-BY-STEP ROADMAP FOR BEGINNERS TO LEARN TO READ, SPEAK, AND UNDERSTAND BASIC SPANISH

VOLUME 1

LANGUAGE ARTS

By L. A. Feliz

www.lafelizbooks.com

DEDICATION

To Daddy, for encouraging me to embrace the Spanish language

To Mommy, for supporting me on my journey with the Spanish language and immersion in the cultures of the Latin world

Para Doña Rosalba García, la cubanita querida que aumentó el fervor y cariño que siento por el español

To my rock, thank you for inspiring me to keep pursuing my dreams

To my beautiful daughter and son, hoping that you will be proud of your Mommy

A Gift for You

+

Get your **FREE** pronunciation guide **AND** your **FREE** copy of

25 Secrets to Master Any Foreign Language

at **lafelizbooks.com**

TABLE OF CONTENTS

INTRODUCTION

I once read a phrase that never had more meaning than when I became a Spanish teacher: "A different language is a different vision of life." This was said by Federico Fellini, an Italian filmmaker who portrayed the greatness and complexity of life through the small lens of his camera. The truth of this phrase became evident to me when I faced the challenge of explaining to a student that "*tendré una ensalada*" is not "I will have a salad." It was not correct to say "*Tendré una ensalada*" at a restaurant because *tener*, "to have" in English, literally means "to possess" in Spanish. Instead of *tener*, she should have used *pedir*, which means "to ask for."

I remember her skeptical look—both feet firmly planted on English-speaking ground. Based on what I explained, she couldn't understand why she couldn't *tener* a salad at a restaurant if she were going to pay for it. The salad was going to be hers, right? Then why was it incorrect to use *tener* if it means "to possess"?

A different language is a different interpretation of life, without a doubt. Behind a language lies certain logic. And this logic is nurtured by social interactions, replicating values, positions, customs, traditions, and much more. So to teach this student how to use *tener* correctly, I had to stand where she was and see life as she did. If there is something I have learned after learning to speak six languages, it is that empathy is the crucial ingredient to enriching any student's language journey. So I descended from my teacher's podium and tried to see the world through her eyes.

From her point of view, the salad was going to be hers. It was for her, and she was paying for it. That's why it was appropriate to tell the waiter, "Yo *tendré una ensalada*," which means "I will have a salad." But when I understood where she was coming from, I let out an "ahh," recognizing and understanding her point of view. After that, she became much more receptive to letting me take her by the hand to the other side of the fence, the side where Spanish was spoken as a first language.

I explained to her that, even if the salad was going to be hers in the future, at the moment of ordering it, it was not. Furthermore, since *tener* literally means "to possess," it would sound strange to say, "I will possess a salad." It would sound as if she was very proud of being the future owner of a salad, and not even the most rigorous vegan would say something like this in English, right? On the other hand, *pedir* ("to ask for" in English) makes more sense in this sentence because it is used to request things.

From a native Spanish speaker's point of view, you are about to order a salad at a restaurant, so it is not yours yet, and people wouldn't usually claim to be the proud owner of a salad. Thus, *pedir* is the most suitable option because it's the one that best fits the context. This logic, applied to this particular context, can also be employed in any other situation. With this criterion, understanding the difference between "to have" and *tener* and how to use this Spanish verb becomes easy, no matter the situation. When my student exclaimed, "Oh!" I knew I had accomplished something. I was able to make a person understand a *different vision of life* for a moment, in other words, to think differently. Moreover, this experience taught me that making parallels between English and Spanish is a valuable tool to help learners assimilate the logic behind the language they want to learn more effectively than making them memorize dull rules.

I have had a lot of rewarding moments like this. Throughout the more than twenty years of teaching Spanish and the more than twenty-five of studying it, I have collected anecdotal moments that have been invaluable to me in developing my teaching methodology and my own system for learning languages. As a student, I have experienced extreme frustration on more than one occasion, as I am sure you have.

The truth is that no matter what level you're at, frustration is a constant in any language journey. But where would we be without frustration? It is there as we grow. When we are children and slowly growing independent of our parents, there will be times when we will experience frustration. Negative emotions are a normal part of growth. Even if you make the same mistake a thousand times, for example, using *por* instead of *para*, it is little mistakes like this that help you on your learning journey.

Before becoming fluent in six languages, I was a beginner in each of them, meaning I have gone through this process six times already. Repetition has enabled me to identify the main barriers that stop us or slow us down when learning. Besides frustration, there is the fear of making mistakes. Why are adults always so afraid of stumbling? We all trip as kids before being able to walk. I have had the opportunity to teach children and adults, and children learn faster than adults every time. Why?

In the beginning, failing now and then is inevitable. If you're afraid of making a mistake, you feel paralyzed and don't do anything. When you are learning a language, practice is vital. During childhood, embarrassment is not part of our vocabulary, and we don't care what people may say. Thus, children repeat everything they have learned to anyone willing to listen to them. If you have children of your own or younger siblings, I am sure you will recognize this scenario: every day, when arriving home from school, they cannot wait to tell you every mind-blowing fact they recently learned about dinosaurs, the earth, plants, and other things in and out of this world. And this actually exercises their memory.

What are you afraid of? As a teacher, one of my priorities is to create a positive classroom environment, meaning my students feel emotionally safe to communicate. Our egos can be quite fragile; therefore, it's essential to be in a class where everyone is tolerant. And practice. Practice everything you learn in this series and from any other source. Who is going to judge you? Native Spanish speakers, happy that a foreigner is trying to learn their language? The foreigner who is fluent after going through the same process you are going through and understands how you feel? The teacher, who is the biggest ally in your language journey?

Open yourself to frustration, rid yourself of your fears by realizing no one is judging you, and grasp the opportunities that your mistakes present. We will start this journey together at stage one, fully mindful of these three maxims. Then, slowly but surely, we will acquire knowledge that is truly useful because it doesn't make sense to learn things you won't feel motivated or eager to use in your daily life.

Do you remember how to calculate the square root of fractions manually? Even if you are an engineer, you probably struggle with remembering how to do it because you use a calculator for most mathematical equations. That's why this series will focus on equipping you with the practical knowledge you need to engage with the aspects of Spanish you love.

In my case, I have always been fond of artistic expression, and I feel passionate about music. What do you love that you wish you could appreciate in Spanish? Literature? Movies? Making friends? Traveling? Whatever it is, we will use it to motivate you in your language journey and steadily remind you of your progress. It's easy to lose focus, so we will constantly tap into that motivation to ensure you reach the necessary milestones at a comfortable pace.

I'm a product of my own methodology, which I have polished over more than two decades of experience fulfilling the roles of teacher and student. This series records every little piece of information I have accumulated, organized in a well-structured, intuitive, and fluid system, so you can smoothly navigate your way towards fluency.

It covers the very basics and puts it in context so that it is meaningful to your life. I'm writing this so you can build a solid foundation with the right set of tools. I hope that later on you can continue to improve your language skills with a genuine grasp of the logic that inspires every grammatical rule and semantic structure. To put it in a nutshell, at the end of this series, you will discover that you *can* speak Spanish.

LA PRIMERA HORA: LENGUAJE Y COMUNICACIÓN
FIRST PERIOD: LANGUAGE ARTS

In this volume, we will navigate through the foundations of Spanish. At the end of this first period, you will be ready to read aloud with proper pronunciation, understand the usage of basic grammar rules, and sustain a simple conversation with native speakers.

Storytime:

¡Buen día! Soy profesora de español y escritora. Tengo un esposo y dos hijos. Amo leer libros. Mi preferido es <u>Cien años de soledad</u> del autor Gabriel García Márquez. Es un libro muy largo y muy interesante.
La historia habla de una familia que vive en el pueblo ficticio de Macondo. ¡El final del libro es increíble! Es una sorpresa para el lector.
¿Cuál es tu libro favorito?

"Wait, what?" If this is your reaction when trying to read the paragraph above, don't worry! You should be able to read this little story by the time we are through with first period. The story will make more sense as you progress through each volume in our series. Before understanding words, we must become acquainted with the letters that make them up. The Spanish alphabet is useful for spelling. The following table will teach you the formal name of these letters, BUT the most important table for pronunciation is the one that comes right after this one, the phonetics table.

PREPARÁNDOSE PARA LEER

GETTING READY TO READ

El alfabeto (The Alphabet)
(stress the syllables that are capitalized)

Spanish Letter	Spanish Name	English Pronunciation	Pronunciation Guide
a	a	ah	Always pronounced "ah" like the a in large
b	be / be larga / be alta / be grande	beh / beh LAR-gah / beh AL-tah / beh GRAHN-deh	Pronounced like a softer version of the English b
c	ce	seh	Before a, o, u, pronounced like k Before e, i, pronounced like s (or th in many parts of Spain and Equatorial Guinea)
ch	che	cheh	Pronounced like the ch in chore (While ch is no longer considered a single letter, note that it is listed after c in older dictionaries.)
d	de	deh	A softer version of the English d, pronounced with the tongue against the top two teeth, as when pronouncing the th in the or then
e	e	eh	Always pronounced "eh" like the e in education
f	efe	EH-feh	Pronounced like the English f

g	ge	heh	Before *a, o, u,* pronounced like *g* Before *e, i,* pronounced like *h* (some pronounce it as a raspy *h,* sometimes noted as "kh")
h	hache	AH-cheh	*H* is always silent, except when it follows *c* for the "ch" sound
i	i (i latina)	ee (ee lah-TEE-nah)	Always pronounced "ee" like the *e* in *hero*
j	jota	HOH-tah	Pronounced like *h* (some pronounce it with a raspy *h,* sometimes noted as "kh")
k	ka	kah	Pronounced like the English *k* (primarily seen in foreign words)
l	ele	EH-leh	Pronounced like the English *l,* but the tongue is raised closer to the roof of the mouth
ll	elle / doble ele	EL-yeh / DOH-bleh EH-leh	Pronounced like the English *y* in many places; also pronounced like the English *j,* the *s* in *leisure,* and *sh* sounds (While *ll* is no longer considered a single letter, note that it is listed after *l* in older dictionaries.)
m	eme	EH-meh	Pronounced like the English *m*
n	ene	EH-neh	Pronounced like the English *n*
ñ	eñe	EH-nyeh	Pronounced like the *gn* in *lasagna*

o	o	oh	Always pronounced "oh" like the o in *hero*
p	pe	peh	A softer version of the English p, with less breath afterward. If it appears before s, the p is silent
q	cu	koo	Q is always followed by the letter u and pronounced like k
r	ere	EH-reh	A softer version of the English r, almost pronounced as a d; at the beginning of words, the r is trilled (or rolled) like the rr
rr	erre	EHR-reh	Pronounced as a trilled or rolling r; it helps to blow air to vibrate the tongue to be able to produce this sound
s	ese	EH-seh	Pronounced like the English s
t	te	teh	A softer version of the English t, with the tongue touching the teeth and no breath afterwards
u	u	oo	Always pronounced like the oo in *school*
v	uve / ve corta / ve chica / ve baja	OO-beh / beh COHR-tah / beh CHEE-kah / beh BAH-hah	Pronounced like a softer version of the English b
w	doble uve / doble ve / doble u / uve doble	DOH-bleh OO-veh / DOH-bleh veh / DOH-bleh oo / OO-veh DOH-bleh	Pronounced like the English w (primarily seen in foreign words)

x	equis	EH-kees	Pronounced like the English x; in names of people and places, especially from Mexico, it can be pronounced like a raspy h, s, or sh
y	ye (i griega)	ye (ee GRYEH-gah)	Pronounced like the English y; when alone, pronounced liked the Spanish i; some pronounce y as the English j
z	zeta	SEH-tah	Mostly pronounced like the English s; pronounced th in many areas of Spain and Equatorial Guinea

Now you know how to spell. To learn how to pronounce Spanish words, we need to understand the phonetics that comes from the combination between vowels and consonants.

The secret to sounding natural when speaking Spanish is... wait for it... VOWELS! How English speakers pronounce vowels differs greatly from how Spanish speakers do so. English vowels have an elongated sound, while Spanish vowels have a short one. English vowels also tend to have more than one sound, but Spanish vowels don't. Additionally, the sound of English vowels can change according to the consonants next to them, but Spanish vowels always preserve their original sound no matter what consonant appears before or after them.

When practicing the combination between vowels and consonants, it is essential to start reading aloud in Spanish, remembering to keep your vowels short and dry. Some combinations are "special," but they only depend on the mix between a specific vowel and a specific consonant, not on the letters around them in a word.

15

Tabla Fonética (Phonetics Table)

Spanish letter	Combinations	Pronunciation Guide
a	(ah)	**Always pronounced "ah" like the *a* in *large***
b	ba be bi bo bu	Pronounced like a softer version of the English *b*
c	ca ce ci co cu	Before *a, o, u*, pronounced like *k* Before *e, i*, pronounced like *s* (or *th* in many parts of Spain and Equatorial Guinea)
ch	cha che chi cho chu	Pronounced like the *ch* in *chore* (While *ch* is no longer considered a single letter, note that it is listed after c in older dictionaries.)
d	da de di do du	A softer version of the English *d*, pronounced with the tongue against the top two teeth, as when pronouncing the *th* in *the* or *then*
e	eh	**Always pronounced "eh" like the *e* in *education***
f	fa fe fi fo fu	Pronounced like the English *f*
g	ga ge gi go gu	Before *a, o, u*, pronounced like *g* Before *e, i*, pronounced like *h* (some pronounce it as a raspy *h*, sometimes noted as "kh")
	gue gui	With *g+u+e or g+u+i*, the *u* is silent, and the sound is the same as the *g* in *ga, go*, and *gu*
	güe güi	With *g+ü+e or g+ü+i*, the *u* must be pronounced. The sound is the same as "*gu+e*" or "*gu+i*"
h	ha he hi ho hu	H is always silent, except when it follows c for the "ch" sound
i	ee	**Always pronounced "ee" like the *e* in *hero***
j	ja je ji jo ju	Pronounced like *h* (some pronounce it with a raspy *h*, sometimes noted as "kh")

k	ka ke ki ko ku	Pronounced like the English *k* (primarily seen in foreign words)
l	la le li lo lu	Pronounced like the English *l*, but the tongue is raised closer to the roof of the mouth
ll	lla lle lli llo llu	Pronounced like the English *y* in many places; also pronounced like the English *j*, the *s* in *leisure*, and *sh* sounds (While *ll* is no longer considered a single letter, note that it is listed after *l* in older dictionaries.)
m	ma me mi mo mu	Pronounced like the English *m*
n	na ne ni no nu	Pronounced like the English *n*
ñ	ña ñe ñi ño ñu	Pronounced like the *gn* in *lasagna*
o	oh	**Always pronounced "oh" like the *o* in *hero***
p	pa pe pi po pu	A softer version of the English *p*, with less breath afterwards If it appears before *s*, the *p* is silent
q	que qui	Q is always followed by the letter *u* and pronounced like *k*. It only has two combinations, *que* and *qui*
r	ra re ri ro ru	When in the middle of the word, it sounds like a softer version of the English *r*, almost pronounced as a *d*
	ra re ri ro ru	When at the beginning of the word, it sounds stronger
	"r" + consonants:	
	bra bre bri bro bru cra cre cri cro cru dra dre dri dro dru fra fre fri fro fru gra gre gri gro gru pra pre pri pro pru tra tre tri tro tru	Combinations with *r* and consonants sound similar to the English ones; the vowels must have a short and dry sound
rr	rra rre rri rro rru	Pronounced as a trilled or rolling *r*; it helps to blow air to vibrate the tongue to be able to produce this sound

s	sa se si so su	Pronounced like the English s
t	ta te ti to tu	A softer version of the English t, with the tongue touching the teeth and no breath afterwards
u	oo	**Always pronounced like the oo in** *school*
v	va ve vi vo vu	Pronounced like a softer version of the English b
w	wa we wi wo wu	Pronounced like the English w (primarily seen in foreign words)
x	xa xe xi xo xu	Pronounced like the English x; in names of people and places, especially from Mexico, it can be pronounced like a raspy h, s, or sh
y	ya ye yi yo yu	Pronounced like the English y; when alone, pronounced liked the Spanish i; some pronounce y as the English j
z	za ze zi zo zu	Mostly pronounced like the English s; pronounced th in many areas of Spain and Equatorial Guinea

After practicing the phonetic table, it's time to see what we've learned so far. And, while we're at it, why not learn some new vocabulary too?

Here's an extra tip. Every word in Spanish can be divided into independent segments (consonant + vowel) and pronounced in blocks since the way they are pronounced is not affected by the rest of the parts of the word. If there is a lone consonant, you can pronounce its raw sound (not the name they have in the alphabet, just the sound, which is similar to the one in English).

For example, say the word "curate" in English. Repeat it using the knowledge we just acquired from the Phonetic Table. Remember, the vowels must have a short and dry sound. This word can be divided as *cu / ra / te*, just a simple combination between consonants and vowels, like the ones we saw in the table above.

Check out this list of words that you'll be able to use in your daily life.

Spanish Letter	Vocabulary	English Meaning	Male Names	Female Names
a	el alumno la alumna el altavoz la aplicación	the male student the female student the speaker the app	Alberto Alejandro	Ana Abril Angelina
b	el bolígrafo	the pen	Benjamín	Berta Blanca
c	la computadora la clase la cámara el coche el carro la carta	the computer the class the camera the car the car / cart the letter / menu	Carlos César	Catalina Carmen Carolina Cristina
ch	el chofer	the driver	Chucho	Chabela
d	el director la directora	the male director/principal the female director/principal	Dante	Dina
e	el equipo el enlace	the team the link	Enrique	Elena Elisabet
f	la forma	the shape	Francisco Fernando Felipe	Fátima Fernanda
g	la goma de borrar el globo la grapadora	the eraser the globe/balloon the stapler	Gerardo Gonzalo	Gabina Gisela
h	el hilo el horario el hombre	the thread the schedule the man	Héctor Hernando	Hada Hilda
i	el instrumento la impresora	the instrument the printer	Igor	Isabel Isla
j	el jugo	the juice	José Jorge	Jimena Josefina
k	el kilo	the kilo	Kevin	Katarina
l	el libro el lápiz	the book the pencil	Lorenzo Lucas	Luz Lola

ll	la llave	the key		Llanet
m	la mochila el morral el micrófono el mapa la mujer	the backpack the satchel the microphone the map the woman	Martín Miguel	María Maya
n	el niño la niña	the boy the girl	Néstor	Nina
ñ	el ñame	the yam	Toño	
o	el ordenador	the computer	Omar Óscar	Olga
p	el pupitre la pared el pegamento la pantalla el portátil	the school desk the wall the glue the screen the laptop	Pablo Pedro	Paca Pepa
q	la química	chemistry	Quique	
r	la regla el reloj el rompecabezas el ratón la red	the ruler the clock the puzzle the computer mouse the internet	Ricardo Roberto	Rosa Rita
rr	el borrador la pizarra	the eraser the board	Curro	Socorro
s	la silla el sacapuntas	the chair the pencil sharpener	Sabino Salomón	Sara Samanta
t	las tijeras el techo el teclado	the scissors the ceiling the keyboard	Tito Tomás	Tamara Teresa
u	el uniforme	the uniform	Ulises	Úrsula
v	la ventana el ventilador de techo la velocidad el volumen	the window the ceiling fan the speed the volume	Valentín Vicente	Vanesa Verónica
w	el wifi	the wifi	Wilfredo	Wendy
x	el xilófono	the xylophone		Ximena
y	el yoga	yoga	Yago	Yadira Yamilet
z	los zapatos	the shoes	Zahid	Zafira

Now, let's polish your pronunciation even more. You already know how to say words by dividing them into blocks, but how do you pronounce two or three vowels in a row? Well, welcome to the fascinating world of Spanish vowels. I wasn't joking when I told you the key to sounding natural lies in these five little elements. Many native English speakers tend to distort sounds composed of "au" or "ia," forgetting our golden rule: all vowels preserve their original raw sound at all times. So let's explore all the possible combinations.

First, we are going to classify our vowels. A, e, and o are considered strong vowels, while i and u are considered weak ones.

NOTE: Always keep in mind that sounds don't merge, especially the sounds of vowels. They transition from one original sound to the other.

- *Diptongos* (Diphthongs)

A *diptongo* is a sequence of two different vowels pronounced in just one syllable. The transition between one vowel to the other should be fast, and the strong ones dominate the final sound. Depending on the components of the *diptongo*, we can have:

a. Strong Vowel + Weak Vowel: Fast transition; the dominant vowel has more presence than the weak one

Strong Vowel + Weak Vowel	*Ejemplos* (Examples)
ai, ay	baile (dance) aire (air) hay (there is)
au	aula (classroom) auto (car) restaurante (restaurant)
ei, ey	seis (six) ley (law)
eu	euro (euro) reunir (to gather)

ia	Asia (Asia) alergia (allergy) memoria (memory)
ie	siete (seven) diez (ten) viento (wind)
io	idioma (language) violeta (violet) biblioteca (library) diccionario (dictionary) ejercicio (exercise)
oi, oy	oigo (I hear) hoy (today)
ua	cuatro (four) cuando (when) usuario (user) cuaderno (notebook)
ue	nueve (nine) sueño (dream) escuela (school) juego (game)
uo	mutuo (mutual) cuota (fee)

b. Weak Vowel + Weak Vowel: Fast transition; neither dominates the *diptongo*

Weak Vowel + Weak Vowel	Ejemplos (Examples)
iu	ciudad (city) viuda (widow)
ui, uy	ruido (noise) juicio (judgment) muy (very)

- *Hiato* (Hiatus)

A *hiato* is a sequence of two vowels pronounced in separate syllables. The pairs are often composed of strong vowels, meaning they cannot overshadow each other during the pronunciation but have an equal presence.

a. Strong vowel + Strong vowel: Pronounce each vowel; the transition is slow.

Strong Vowel + Strong Vowel	Ejemplos (Examples)
ae	traer (to bring) maestra / maestro (teacher) aeropuerto (airport)
ao	Paola (the name *Paola*) cacao (cocoa)
ea	marea (tide) teatro (theater) tarea (homework / task)
eo	ateo (atheist) deseo (wish)
oa	canoa (canoe) toalla (towel)
oe	coeficiente (coefficient) poema (poem)

b. Same pair of vowels: Some are divided by "h" (silent). Pronounce each vowel; the transition is slow.

Strong Vowel + Strong Vowel	Ejemplos (Examples)
aa	azahar (orange blossom) albahaca (basil)

ee	leer (to read) creer (to believe)
ii	antiinflamatorio (anti-inflammatory)
oo	zoo (zoo) cooperar (to cooperate) alcohol (alcohol)

c. Strong vowel + Weak vowel with an accent: Accents transform weak vowels into strong ones. Pronounce each vowel; the transition is slow.

Strong Vowel + Weak Vowel	Ejemplos (Examples)
aí	país (country) maíz (corn)
aú	ataúd (coffin) aún (still)
eí	increíble (incredible) reír (to laugh)
eú	transeúnte (passerby) Seúl (Seoul)
ía	día (day) María (Mary)
íe	fríen ((they / you all) fry) ríes (you laugh)
ío	período (period) judío (Jewish)
oí	oír (to hear) roído (gnawed)
oú	noúmeno (noumenon)
úa	grúa (crane) cacatúa (cockatoo)
úe	iglúes (igloos) hindúes (Hindus)
úo	flúor (fluoride) búho (owl)

- *Triptongos* (Triphthongs)

Triptongos are sequences of three vowels that are pronounced in just one syllable. They always follow this formula: weak vowel + strong vowel + weak vowel. The transition is fast, and the strong vowel works as an anchor, tying the other two sounds together. When you pronounce a *triptongo*, think about a roller coaster: keep it low with the first weak vowel, then go up with the strong one, and then go back down with the third weak one. You must stress the strong vowel. Don't combine the sounds; pronounce each of them.

Weak Vowel + Strong Vowel + Weak Vowel	*Ejemplos* (Examples)
iai	estudiáis (you all study)
iei	estudiéis (you all may study)
uai, uay	continuáis (you all continue) Uruguay (Uruguay)
uei, uey	continuéis (you all may continue) buey (ox)

We are clear now about the principles of pronouncing words with two or three vowels in a row. Let's move on to a fascinating topic: the accent. Accents are little hats that can be placed on top of vowels, only once per word, and they obey specific grammatical rules that we won't delve into now. For now, their presence or absence is important to us to help us know what part of the word we must stress when pronouncing it.

Remember we can divide words into blocks? Let's call those blocks *syllables*. Syllables can be a mix between a consonant and a vowel or two consonants and one vowel. A syllable can also be composed of just one strong vowel. We always form them from left to right.

Let's look at some simple rules for this.

- If a consonant is between vowels: the consonant pairs with the vowel following it.

  > ola (wave) → o - la
  > hilo (thread) → hi - lo
  > olor (smell) → o - lor

- If two consonants are between vowels: the first consonant pairs with the vowel before it, and the second one pairs with the one following it.

  > formas (shapes) → for - mas
  > Carlos → Car - los
  > Berta → Ber - ta

- If two consonants can't be separated because they form a cluster, the consonant cluster pairs with the vowel following it.

  > clase (class) → cla - se
  > chofer (driver) → cho - fer
  > equipo (team) → e - qui - po

- If three consonants lie between vowels, the first two consonants pair with the preceding vowel, and the third one pairs with the vowel following it.

  > instinto (instinct) → ins - tin - to

- If there are three consonants but the last two form a cluster, the consonant cluster pairs with the vowel following it.

  > engrapadora (stapler) → en - gra - pa - do - ra
  > impresora (printer) → im - pre - so -ra

- If there are four consonants between vowels, the first two pair with the preceding vowel, and the two that form the cluster pair with the vowel following them.

construir (to build) → cons - truir

transplante (transplant) → trans - plan - te

instrucción (instruction) → ins - truc - ción

- Each strong vowel forms a syllable if there are two strong vowels in a row.

ateo (atheist) → a - te - o

canoa (canoe) → ca - no - a

toalla (towel) → to - a - lla

- If two weak vowels or a weak one and a strong one are together, they cannot be separated.

ciudad (city) → ciu - dad

nueve (nine) → nue - ve

país (country) → país

- If h and x are between vowels, they pair with the second vowel.

examen (exam) → e - xa - men

ahorros (savings) → a - ho - rros

Check out this table with more examples!

Palabra (Word)	Significado (Meaning)	Sílabas (Syllables)
mar	sea	mar (one syllable)
luz	light	luz (one syllable)
sol	sun	sol (one syllable)
rey	king	rey (one syllable)
mil	one thousand	mil (one syllable)
árbol	tree	ár/bol (two syllables)
aire	air	ai/re (two syllables)
antes	before	an/tes (two syllables)
banco	bank	ban/co (two syllables)
casa	house	ca/sa (two syllables)
peligro	danger	pe/li/gro (three syllables)
abrazo	hug	a/bra/zo (three syllables)
amigo	friend	a/mi/go (three syllables)
cabeza	head	ca/be/za (three syllables)
escribir	to write	es/cri/bir (three syllables)
alegría	joy	a/le/grí/a (four syllables)
aéreo	aerial	a/é/re/o (four syllables)
empleado	employee	em/ple/a/do (four syllables)
habitación	bedroom	ha/bi/ta/ción (four syllables)
película	movie	pe/lí/cu/la (four syllables)
capitalismo	capitalism	ca/pi/ta/lis/mo (five syllables)
ecológico	ecological	e/co/ló/gi/co (five syllables)
fotografía	photograph	fo/to/gra/fí/a (five syllables)
interesante	interesting	in/te/re/san/te (five syllables)
oportunidad	opportunity	o/por/tu/ni/dad (five syllables)

Your turn! Divide these words into syllables to practice your pronunciation.

Palabra (Word)	Significado (Meaning)	Sílabas (Syllables)
voz	voice	
limón	lemon	
horario	schedule	
libro	book	
reloj	clock	
yoga	yoga	
Quique	Quique (name)	
Igor	Igor (name)	
sueño	dream	
albahaca	basil	
cooperar	to cooperate	
período	period	
búho	owl	
grúa	crane	
Uruguay	Uruguay	

Are you getting the idea? Now, let's talk about the formal name of the syllables from right to left. The ultimate, or final, syllable is always the one closing the word. The penultimate syllable is right before the ultimate one, and the antepenultimate syllable is right before the penultimate syllable. Those three syllables are the ones that usually have accents. For example, in the word *película*, "*la*" is the ultimate syllable, "*cu*" is the penultimate one, and "*li*" is the antepenultimate syllable.

Alright. Now that we have kicked that out of the way, let's talk about accents and pronunciation.

- When words have **no** accents:

  a. Words ending in *n*, *s*, or a vowel → stress the penultimate syllable

    - examen (exam)
    - sacapuntas (pencil sharpener)
    - hola (hello)

  b. Words ending in a consonant (except *n* or *s*) without a written accent → stress the last syllable

    - borrador (eraser)
    - papel (paper)
    - hablar (to speak)

- When words have accents, called *tildes* in Spanish, always stress the syllable that contains the *tilde*.

  a. Words with *tildes* where the stress doesn't lie where it does normally

    - lápiz (pencil)
    - bolígrafo (pen)
    - página (page)

  b. Words that are spelled the same, but have different meanings with or without *tildes*.

    - si (if) vs. sí (yes)

  Si ganas el partido, saldré contigo. = If you win the match, I will go out with you.

  Sí, quiero comer algo. = Yes, I want to eat something.

- *el* (the) vs. *él* (he)

El televisor es grande. = The TV is big.

Él es una buena persona. = He is a good person.

- *se* (reflexive pronoun) vs. *sé* (I know)

Se lava los dientes. = He/She/You (formal) wash/es his/her/ your teeth.

No sé. = I don't know.

- *te* (you - object pronoun) vs. *té* (tea)

Te pagaré. = I will pay you.

Bebo té. = I drink tea.

- *tu* (your) vs. *tú* (you - subject pronoun)

María es tu hermana. = María is your sister.

Tú eres alta. = You are tall.

- When words are adverbs:

While English adverbs usually end in -*lly*, Spanish adverbs typically end in -*mente*. To pronounce them correctly, divide them into two parts—the root adjective (which has a feminine ending—more details about what *feminine* refers to will come later on) and -*mente*. Stress the adjective as if it were standing alone, and then pronounce -*mente* stressing -*men*-. Basically, adverbs ending in -*mente* receive stress in two spots. It's easier than you think! The following examples have the stressed syllables underlined.

- <u>len</u>ta<u>men</u>te (slowly)
- <u>rá</u>pida<u>men</u>te (quickly)
- co<u>rrec</u>ta<u>men</u>te (correctly)

31

COGNADOS

COGNATES

Time to talk about *cognados*. Although English is a Germanic language and Spanish is a Romance one, they share some similarities. Therefore, some Spanish words may sound familiar to you. That's because they share the same meaning as the English words they resemble. This makes *cognados* easy to remember, and that's why they are a great addition to your vocabulary.

Spanish	English
no	no
clase	class
gimnasio	gym/gymnasium
oficina	office
profesor	professor
estudiante	student
vacación	vacation
matemáticas	mathematics
biología	biology
historia	history
examen	exam

Falsos Cognados (False Cognates)

On the other hand, we have a category of words that resemble one thing in English but mean something entirely different in Spanish. *Falsos cognados* are also known as *Falsos amigos* (false friends) because only a terrible friend would put you through the social stress one of these words can put you through. But, of course, they also make for anecdotal situations that we can look back on later with a smile on our faces. Ah, the wonderful path towards fluency is rocky, but it is always full of laughter!

Let me tell you a little story so we can avoid using two of the false cognates that torment foreign speakers the most during their first conversational encounters. I was teaching a class one day, and we were going to perform a role-play exercise. One of my students was going to pretend his birthday was that day, and my other student was going to pretend she was congratulating him on his birthday. Everything went well until she wanted to apologize for not bringing him a gift as part of her role-play. So she said:

- Lo siento mucho, no tengo un regalo por tu cumpleaños. ¡Estoy tan **embarazada!**

So the first part means: "I'm very sorry, I don't have a gift for your birthday." What do you think the second part means? You probably read the word *embarazada* and thought "embarrassed." Well, that's the first false cognate we need to learn! *Embarazada* means "pregnant" in Spanish. *Avergonzada* (for females) or *avergonzado* (for males) is the correct way to say "embarrassed." Things got even more entertaining when my other student responded to her as part of his role:

- ¡No hay problema! Gracias por tus felicitaciones, estoy muy **excitado.**

And so, my student used the second false cognate. The first part means: "There is no problem! Thank you for your congratulations. I'm very..." And then, what do you think *excitado* sounds like? "Excited," right? Well, it sounds like it, but it actually means "turned on." So... yeah, my first student basically said she was very pregnant, and my second one... well, you get the idea. The correct word for "excited" is *emocionado* (for males) or *emocionada* (for females).

How did I correct them after the exercise? With a huge smile! Moments like this make teaching and learning fun. Mistakes are made by everybody all the time, and the only thing left to do is embrace them and enjoy them. After all, they are precious learning opportunities.

33

PREPARÁNDOSE PARA HABLAR

PREPARING TO SPEAK

Good job so far! You have reached the part of the book where we start learning our first phrases to begin conversing with other Spanish speakers. Let's start by explaining a little bit about formal and informal ways. Spanish has two different pronouns for "you."

For the informal "you," we use *tú*. *Tú* is used to address peers, people we have a certain level of familiarity with, friends, family, or younger people.

For the formal "you," we use *usted*. *Usted* is used to address people older than us, people we don't know, a superior such as a boss, or just someone to whom you want to demonstrate respect.

Why is this important? Because Spanish verbs are conjugated with each pronoun. Although in English, it's enough to put the pronoun first and then the verb (e.g., *you run*), in Spanish, we have two different endings for the verb depending on whether we use the informal or formal "you" (e.g., *Tú corres / Usted corre*).

Hey! Don't overthink it. We will talk more about it when it is time. Right now, this is just a helpful explanation to understand why you will see a formal and informal way to say the following phrases.

- *Saludos* (Greetings)

English	Spanish
Hello!	¡Hola!
Hi!	¡Buenas!
Good morning!	¡Buenos días!
Good afternoon!	¡Buenas tardes!

- *Bienestar* (Well-being)

English Phrase	Informal Spanish	Formal Spanish
How are you?	¿Cómo estás?	¿Cómo está?
What's up?	¿Qué tal?	x
Well, thank you	Bien, gracias	
Very well	Muy bien	
And you?	¿Y tú? ¿Y vos?*	¿Y usted?

*Vos is another informal way to say "you" used by some Spanish-speaking countries. More details about using *vos* will come later.

- *Presentándose* (Introducing Oneself)

English Phrase	Informal Spanish	Formal Spanish
What's your name?	¿Cuál es tu nombre?	¿Cuál es su nombre?
My name is...	Mi nombre es...	
What's your name? (How are you called?)	¿Cómo te llamas?	¿Cómo se llama?
My name is... (I'm called...)	Me llamo...	
I'm...	Soy...	
And you?	¿Y tú? ¿Y vos?	¿Y usted?
Nice to meet you (much pleasure)	Mucho gusto	
It's a pleasure	Es un placer	

Nice to meet you (enchanted)	Encantado (for male) Encantada (for female)
The pleasure is mine	El gusto es mío / El placer es mío
Likewise (equally)	Igualmente

- *Despidiéndose* (Saying Goodbye)

Despedidas (Goodbyes)	Informal Spanish	Formal Spanish
Farewell!/Goodbye!	¡Adiós!	
Good evening!	¡Buenas noches!	
Good night!	¡Buenas noches!	
Bye!	¡Chao!	
See you later!	¡Hasta luego!	
Until next time!	¡Hasta la próxima vez!	
See you tomorrow!	¡Hasta mañana!	
See you soon!	¡Hasta pronto!	
We'll see each other soon!	¡Nos vemos!	

Hey! Did you notice that Spanish uses inverted exclamation and question marks? The reason is quite simple: we like to distinguish statements from questions and exclamations from the beginning in Spanish. Is the intonation any different? It is. But just a little. Accentuate the question or exclamation when you start saying it and when you end it.

Now, let's see three different types of conversations applying what we just learned:

- Conversation 1 → two people speaking formally

Josefina: ¡Hola!
Alberto:¡Hola, buenos días!
Josefina: ¿Cómo está?
Alberto:Muy bien, gracias. ¿Y usted?
Josefina: Bien, gracias.
Alberto:¿Cómo se llama?
Josefina: Me llamo Josefina, ¿y usted?
Alberto:Mi nombre es Alberto.
Josefina: Mucho gusto.
Alberto:El gusto es mío.
Josefina: ¡Adiós!
Alberto:¡Hasta luego!

- Conversation 2 → two people speaking informally

Roberto: ¡Buenas!
Isla: ¡Hola!
Roberto: ¿Cómo estás?
Isla: Bien, gracias. ¿Y tú?
Roberto: Muy bien.
Isla: ¿Cómo te llamas?
Roberto: Me llamo Roberto. ¿Cuál es tu nombre?
Isla: Mi nombre es Isla.
Roberto: Es un placer.
Isla: El placer es mío.
Roberto: ¡Nos vemos!
Isla: ¡Chao!

- Conversation 3 → one person speaking informally addressing a younger person; the second person speaking formally addressing an older unknown person

Gabriela:	¡Hola!
Ricardo:	¡Buenos días!
Gabriela:	¿Cómo estás?
Ricardo:	Muy bien, gracias. Y usted, ¿cómo está?
Gabriela:	Bien, gracias.
Ricardo:	¿Cómo se llama?
Gabriela:	Me llamo Gabriela. Y tú, ¿cómo te llamas?
Ricardo:	Me llamo Ricardo.
Gabriela:	Encantada.
Ricardo:	Igualmente.
Gabriela:	¡Hasta pronto!
Ricardo:	¡Adiós!

EXPLORANDO LA GRAMÁTICA

DIGGING INTO GRAMMAR

Do you remember how your mother loved to dress you in matchy-matchy outfits when you were little? I'm a parent, and I sure stick to the tradition. A similar thing happens in Spanish grammar. Once you have a noun, everything else must match it in gender and number.

Géneros (Genders)

Let's start talking about nouns and genders. In Spanish, every noun has a gender. Some nouns reflect a physical gender. For example, mom and dad are *mamá* and *papá* in Spanish. *Mamá* is a female noun because it refers to a woman, while *papá* is a masculine word because it refers to a man. The same thing happens with "boy" and "girl," which are *niño* and *niña* in Spanish.

But, what happens with nouns that refer to objects or places? In Spanish, objects and places also have genders. And they don't depend on anything else but grammatical rules. The endings of the words let us know what gender they have.

- *Terminaciones de sustantivos masculinos*
  (Masculine noun endings)

Terminaciones (Endings)	Spanish	English
-o	el bolígrafo el libro	the pen the book
Accented vowels -á, -é, -í, -ó, -ú	el sofá el café el ajonjolí el dominó el menú	the sofa the coffee the sesame the domino the menu

Words of Greek origin ending in: -ma, -pa, -ta	el problema el mapa el cometa	the problem the map the comet
Consonants other than *d* and *z*	el árbol el rumor	the tree the rumor
-e	el coche el chocolate	the car the chocolate

Exceptions
(Feminine words with common masculine noun endings)

Terminaciones (Endings)	Spanish	English
-o	la foto la mano la radio	the photo the hand the radio
Consonants other than *d* and *z*	la flor la labor la miel la piel	the flower the labor the honey the skin
-e	la clase la llave la calle	the class the key the street

Exceptions happen all the time in Spanish, but don't let this discourage you. Learn the basic rules first. You will learn the exceptions little by little until it becomes intuitive. Practice and exposure to Spanish will make it easier as time passes. That's how most of us learn a new language anyway—with time and patience!

- *Terminaciones de sustantivos femeninos*
  (Feminine noun endings)

Terminaciones (Endings)	Spanish	English
-a	la computadora la alumna	the computer the female student
-d	la ciudad la felicidad	the city the happiness
-z	la luz la nuez la paz	the light the nut the peace
-ón	la canción la lección la televisión la razón	the song the lesson the television the reason
-umbre	la legumbre la costumbre	the legume the custom

Exceptions
(Masculine words with common feminine noun endings)

Terminaciones (Endings)	Spanish	English
-a	el idioma el día el tema	the language the day the theme / song
-d	el césped el ataúd	the grass / lawn the coffin
-z	el lápiz el pez	the pencil the fish
-ón	el avión el camión	the plane the truck

Again, there are some exceptions to identify the female gender of words. Most of the time, words having these endings are feminine, but there are a few exceptions to the rule.

Número (Number)

Now, it's time to learn the rules to transform singular words into plural ones. To achieve this, you only need to identify the endings of the words and, according to this, add to them or modify them a little bit.

- Vowel ending → Add "s"

Singular	Plural	English Meaning
el estudiante	los estudiantes	(the student/s)
la computadora	las computadoras	(the computer/s)
la directora	las directoras	(the female director/s / principal/s)
el horario	los horarios	(the schedule/s)
la silla	las sillas	(the chair/s)
la mesa	las mesas	(the table/s)

- Consonant ending (other than "z") → Add "es"

Singular	Plural	English Meaning
el director	los directores	(the male director/s / principal/s)
el limón	los limones	(the lemon/s)
la pared	las paredes	(the wall/s)
la red	las redes	(the net/s)
el color	los colores	(the color/s)

- "Z" ending → Drop "z" and add "ces"

Singular	Plural	English Meaning
el lápiz	los lápices	(the pencil/s)
la luz	las luces	(the light/s)
la nuez	las nueces	(the nut/s)
el pez	los peces	(the fish)

- Singular objects that are always plural in form

Singular	Plural	English Meaning
los pantalones	los pantalones	(the pair/s of pants)
las tijeras	las tijeras	(the pair/s of scissors)
los lentes / los anteojos / las gafas	los lentes / los anteojos / las gafas	(the pair/s of glasses)

Artículos (Articles)

Articles are another essential element of basic Spanish grammar; they must match the noun. There are two categories of them: definite and indefinite articles. The thing with articles is that Spanish native speakers love to include them in everything! Or so it seems... because there are exceptions to their usage. We will learn the exceptions little by little, but first, let's see the two categories of articles.

- Definite articles refer to nouns whose identity is known to the listener or reader.

In English, the definite article is just "the." In Spanish, we have four options depending on the word's gender and number.

	Singular	Plural
Masculine	el	los
Feminine	la	las

- Indefinite articles refer to nouns whose identity is unknown by the listener or reader.

In English, the indefinite article is "a." In Spanish, we have four options depending on the word's gender and number.

	Singular	Plural
Masculine	un	unos
Feminine	una	unas

Exceptions

When definite and indefinite articles are *not* necessary:

a. Proper names

- You don't need to use any article when you talk about a person or refer to them by calling them by their name.

> María es buena. = María is good.
> Luis es guapo. = Luis is handsome.

- If you refer to the name of a country or city, you don't need to use an article either.

> Perú es bonito. = Peru is beautiful.
> Brasil es grande. = Brazil is big.

- You do need the articles when talking about rivers, seas, mountains, lakes, volcanos, and similar natural formations. When referring to them by their proper name, however, you must use the definite article corresponding to the noun they refer to.

> El río es grande. = The river is big.
> El Mississippi es grande. = The Mississippi is big.

- You need the masculine definite article when talking about a language. Notice I said "talking about," not referring to it indirectly (like, "I study Spanish.").

> El español es fácil. = Spanish is easy.
> Estudio portugués. = I study Portuguese.

b. No definite article after the verb *haber*, which means "there is; there are"

- We will discuss the significance of this verb, *haber*, later on. But, for now, let's remember that we don't ever use definite articles (*el, los, la, las*) after *haber*.

c. When referring to generic or unspecified plural things

- Generic things don't need articles. For example, suppose you say you want to eat pasta. In that case, you are talking about a generic category (food) and not something specific, like lasagna from your favorite restaurant (a little more precise) or the best pizza in the world (very specific). We would say:

> Quiero comer pasta. = I want to eat pasta.

d. Months

- We don't need articles in front of months:

> Mi cumpleaños es en abril. = My birthday is in April.

e. Professions or occupations

- Usually, professions and occupations are generic, unless you want to say you are the best, I don't know, Spanish teacher in the world—otherwise, no need for articles.

> Soy profesora. = I'm a teacher.
> Soy abogado. = I'm a lawyer.

f. Nationality

- That's right! No articles before nationalities.

> Soy peruana. = I'm Peruvian.
> Soy estadounidense. = I'm American (from the United States).

g. Subjects

- We do not use articles before subjects like math, languages, science, etc.

> Yo estudio español. = I study Spanish.

Alright! It's time to test what you have learned so far. We are going to do some exercises. I will help you with the first one. Remember, EVERYTHING needs to match the noun. Verbs, articles, and adjectives related to a noun need to match it in gender and number. For now, let's just match definite and indefinite articles to nouns in gender and number.

SINGULAR House Vocabulary

Singular in Spanish	English	Definite article	Indefinite article
casa	house	la	una
puerta	door		
entrada	entrance		
pasillo	hallway		
pared	wall		
ventana	window		

piso	floor		
techo	roof		
luz	light		
dormitorio	bedroom		
habitación	bedroom / room		
cuarto	bedroom / room		
cocina	kitchen		
sala	living room		
comedor	dining room		
baño	bathroom		
terraza	terrace / balcony		
patio	patio		
porche	porch		
sótano	basement		
ático	attic		
garaje	garage		
jardín	garden		
césped	grass / lawn		
flor	flower		

Now, complete the next table transforming the singular nouns from before into their plural version. Again, repetition will help you add these new words to your vocabulary.

PLURAL House Vocabulary

Plural in Spanish	English	Definite article	Indefinite article

And now, we will discuss some exceptions. Spanish is a very phonetic language, so it doesn't like "ugly" sounds. For example, we can't use the feminine singular article *la* with a word that starts with "a" or "ha." So, what do we do then? We must change the feminine singular article *la* to the masculine singular article *el*.

So, instead of *la agua* (the water), we have *el agua*.

Instead of *la alma* (the soul), we have *el alma*.

Instead of *la hacha* (the ax), we have *el hacha*.

If these words are plural, we can go back to using the female article since its plural form doesn't sound "ugly" in conjunction with a word starting with a phonetic "a" anymore. So, we have *las aguas* (the waters), *las almas* (the souls), and *las hachas* (the axes).

Pronombres (Pronouns)

I'm very excited you have come this far already! We are getting closer and closer to being able to form coherent, complete, and structured sentences in Spanish. At this point, we really need to use our memory. We will learn the main pronouns used in most Spanish-speaking countries, as well as the specific pronouns used in particular Spanish-speaking countries. At the end of this section, you will see a table with the general pronouns you can use.

- I → yo
- informal you → tú

Most Spanish-speaking countries use *tú* as an informal "you" to refer to peers, family, friends, younger people, and anybody with whom they have a close or casual relationship. These countries are Cuba, the Dominican Republic, Equatorial Guinea, Mexico, Peru, Puerto Rico, and Spain.

- informal you → vos

Vos is also an informal "you," but it's used in Argentina, Costa Rica, El Salvador, Guatemala, Honduras, Nicaragua, Paraguay, and Uruguay.

Some countries use both *tú* and *vos*, such as Bolivia, Chile, Colombia, Ecuador, Panama, and Venezuela.

- formal you → usted

Usted is a pronoun used to refer to people we want to show respect to, whether we are obliged to by social norms or hierarchy. You can use *usted* to refer to your boss, an elder, someone you have a very formal relationship with, or someone you don't know. The abbreviation that is used for *usted* is Ud.

- he → él
- she → ella
- they (all males) → ellos

When referring to a group of people who are all males, we use *ellos*.

- they (all females) → ellas

On the other hand, if the group we refer to is composed of only females, we use *ellas*.

- they (mixed group) → ellos

When we refer to a mixed group comprising both female and male members, we use the masculine plural form by default. This rule applies to any other group composed of people of both sexes.

- you all (all-female, all-male, or mixed group) → ustedes

Ustedes is the word Spanish-speaking countries other than Spain and Equatorial Guinea use to address a group informally and formally. It can be a group composed of all males, all females, or both. In Spain and Equatorial Guinea, this form is only used formally. The abbreviation that is used for *ustedes* is Uds.

- you all (all males) → vosotros

Vosotros is the form used in Spain and Equatorial Guinea to address a group of all males informally.

- you all (all females) → vosotras

Vosotras is the form used in Spain and Equatorial Guinea to address a group of all females informally.

- you all (mixed group) → vosotros

When we refer to a mixed group with female and male members, we use the masculine plural form.

- we (all males) → nosotros

When we refer to "us" as a group consisting of only males, we use *nosotros*.

- we (all females) → nosotras

When we refer to "us" as a group of only females, we use *nosotras*.

- we (mixed group) → nosotros

We always use the masculine plural form by default when we refer to "us" as a group with both female and male members. This rule applies to any other group composed of people of both sexes.

So now you know the different pronouns used in different countries. The following table organizes the pronouns in a way that will prepare us for using them in forming a sentence.

Pronouns	Pronombres
I	yo
you (informal) [most used]	tú
you (informal in some countries)	vos
he / she / you (formal)	él / ella / usted
we (masculine) / we (feminine)	nosotros / nosotras
you all (informal from Spain)	vosotros / vosotras
they (masculine) / they (feminine) / you all (informal & formal)	ellos / ellas / ustedes

Verbos (Verbs)

Guess what... we have reached that part where we start forming sentences! Are you excited? This section will contain more exercises to practice what you have been learning. Ready? Let's jump into the theory first so you can then sharpen your skills in the practice section.

- *Infinitivo* (Infinitive)

Just as in English, the infinitive is the original form of a verb. The infinitive is the non-conjugated verb (so it is not in conjunction with any pronoun), and it doesn't express any particular time (in a timeline, it doesn't express present, past, or future; it's not a conditional or a command).

The infinitive is important in Spanish because it lets us categorize verbs. Contrary to English, all verbs in Spanish in their original form, i.e., the infinitive, can have three different endings: *-ar*, *-er*, *-ir*. And only those three. Let's see some examples:

- to love → amar
- to run → correr
- to live → vivir

So, while the infinitive in English is expressed by "to + *verb*," in Spanish, it is expressed by verbs ending in -*ar*, -*er*, -*ir*.

Verbs ending in -*ar* are in the First Conjugation category.

Verbs ending in -*er* are in the Second Conjugation category.

Verbs ending in -*ir* are in the Third Conjugation category.

"Why are the categories important?" you may wonder. Ah, I'm glad you asked! To conjugate verbs (that is, to use them with a pronoun), Spanish has rules that depend on the termination of the verb. In English, if you want to transform the infinitive "to love" into the present tense, you just need to change the "to" into a pronoun. In Spanish, you need to change the ending of the infinitive (-*ar*, -*er*, -*ir*) into another one according to the category the verb belongs to AND the pronoun you want to use.

Don't worry, it will make more sense once we see some examples.

First, we will see the rules for the regular verbs. "Regular" means that the rules are the same for every verb that belongs to the first, second, or third conjugation.

- *Presente indicativo* (Present Indicative)

The *indicativo* is a group of verb tenses that refers to any concrete actions, that is, actions that happened, happen, or will happen. The present tense in Spanish is used the same way as in English. However, you can also use it to talk about routines, actions, or events that happen daily or commonly.

Here is a table that will help us understand how conjugating verbs in the present tense works in Spanish. I'm including all of the specific pronouns used in different Spanish-speaking countries, but keep in mind that the pronouns labeled "optional" are not used by most of Latin America:

Pronombres (Pronouns)	1st conjugation: -ar	2nd conjugation: -er	3rd conjugation: -ir
yo	-o	-o	-o
tú	-as	-es	-es
vos (optional)	-ás	-és	-ís
él / ella / usted	-a	-e	-e
nosotros / nosotras	-amos	-emos	-imos
vosotros / vosotras (optional)	-áis	-éis	-ís
ellos / ellas / ustedes	-an	-en	-en

As you can see, there are four columns: the first is for the pronouns, and the other three correspond to the three categories verbs can belong to according to their ending. If you want to conjugate a verb that belongs to the 1st conjugation with the pronoun *yo*, then you have to change the end, -ar, to -o.

We are going to use the following verbs: *amar* (to love), which belongs to the first conjugation; *correr* (to run), which belongs to the second conjugation; and *vivir* (to live), which belongs to the third conjugation. Let's see how we apply the rules in the following table.

Pronombres (Pronouns)	amar	correr	vivir
yo	amo	corro	vivo
tú	amas	corres	vives
vos (optional)	amás	corrés	vivís
él / ella / usted	ama	corre	vive
nosotros / nosotras	amamos	corremos	vivimos

vosotros / vosotras (optional)	amáis	corréis	vivís
ellos / ellas / ustedes	aman	corren	viven

See? We just replaced the ending, or suffix if we want to be fancier, for any of the options given per pronoun. Now, try it!

Pronombres (Pronouns)	hablar (to speak/talk)	aprender (to learn)	escribir (to write)
yo			
tú			
vos			
él / ella / usted			
nosotros / nosotras			
vosotros / vosotras			
ellos / ellas / ustedes			

Pronombres (Pronouns)	estudiar (to study)	leer (to read)	recibir (to receive)
yo			
tú			
vos			
él / ella / usted			
nosotros / nosotras			

vosotros / vosotras			
ellos / ellas / ustedes			

Pronombres (Pronouns)	mirar (to look)	comer (to eat)	compartir (to share)
yo			
tú			
vos			
él / ella / usted			
nosotros / nosotras			
vosotros / vosotras			
ellos / ellas / ustedes			

Pronombres (Pronouns)	enseñar (to teach)	creer (to believe)	persuadir (to persuade)
yo			
tú			
vos			
él / ella / usted			
nosotros / nosotras			
vosotros / vosotras			
ellos / ellas / ustedes			

Now, we will learn our first useful phrases. We will use some of the verbs that we just learned:

- Useful phrases with *hablar*:

Hablo inglés.	(I speak English.)
¿Hablas inglés?	(Do you (informal) speak English?)
¿Habla español?	(Do you (formal) speak Spanish?)
Hablamos inglés y español.	(We speak English and Spanish.)

- Useful phrases with *estudiar*:

Estudio español.	(I study Spanish.)
¿Estudias español? Sí, estudio español.	(Do you (informal) study Spanish?) (Yes, I study Spanish.)
¿Estudia español? Sí, estudio español.	(Do you (formal) study Spanish?) (Yes, I study Spanish.)
Estudiamos español.	(We study Spanish.)
¿Estudiáis español? Sí, estudiamos español.	(Do you (all) study Spanish?) (Yes, we study Spanish.)
¿Estudian español? Sí, estudiamos español.	(Do you (all) study Spanish?) (Yes, we study Spanish.)

- Useful phrases with *enseñar*:

Enseño en la primaria.	(I teach in primary school.)
Enseño en la secundaria.	(I teach in middle/high school.)
Enseño en el colegio.	(I teach in school.)
Enseño en la universidad.	(I teach in university.)
¿Enseñas? No, estudio.	(Do you (informal) teach?) (No, I study.)

¿Usted enseña?	(Do you (formal) teach?)
Sí, enseño inglés.	(Yes, I teach English.)
Enseñamos inglés.	(We teach English.)
¿Vosotras enseñáis?	(Do you (all females) teach?)
Sí, enseñamos inglés.	(Yes, we teach English.)
¿Ustedes enseñan?	(Do you all teach?)
Sí, enseñamos inglés.	(Yes, we teach English.)

- Useful phrases with *leer*:

Leo inglés.	(I read English.)
¿Lees inglés?	(Do you (informal) read English?)
No, leo español.	(No, I read Spanish.)
¿Lee inglés?	(Do you (formal) read English?)
Sí, leo inglés.	(Yes, I read English.)
Leemos español.	(We read Spanish.)
¿Leéis inglés?	(Do you all read English?)
No, leemos español.	(No, we read Spanish.)
¿Leen inglés?	(Do you all read English?)
Sí, leemos inglés.	(Yes, we read English.)

- Useful phrases with *escribir*:

¿Escribes un mensaje de texto?	(Are you (informal) writing a text message?)
Sí, escribo un mensaje de texto.	(Yes, I am writing a text message.)
Ella escribe un email.	(She's writing an email.)
¿Escribe un email?	(Are you (formal) writing an email?)
Sí, escribo un email.	(Yes, I am writing an email.)

NOTE: Since every noun has its own ending, native Spanish speakers generally don't use the pronoun and the verb together, only the verb. The conjugated verbs already denote what pronouns they are using, so it's not necessary to use the pronoun. But it's better to use the pronoun if we want to make sure the person we are talking with understands whom we are referring to. For example, *él*, *ella*, and *usted* use the same suffixes, so if we say, "*Corre rápido*" (he/she/you formal run/s fast), the other person would need context to be able to distinguish the pronoun we are conjugating *correr* with.

Ser and *Estar* (To Be)

You may be wondering why we didn't include "to be" in the Present Indicative section. The verb "to be" requires its own space because Spanish uses two different verbs with different meanings for "to be."

– To be → *Ser*

Ser is an irregular verb, meaning it doesn't follow the rules we reviewed before for the present tense. This is how you have to conjugate *ser*:

Pronombres (Pronouns)	*ser* (to be)
yo	soy
tú	eres
vos (optional)	sos
él / ella / usted	es
nosotros / nosotras	somos
vosotros / vosotras (optional)	sois
ellos / ellas / ustedes	son

We use *ser* to talk about a stable attribute that exists, existed, or will exist. At the moment of speaking, this attribute seems relatively permanent and doesn't give the idea of changing any time soon. What characteristics come to mind? Personality traits, adjectives related to height, nationalities, professions, etc. Let's check the following table to get a better idea of what we can use *ser* for:

Usage	Examples
Características (Characteristics)	La casa es grande. (The house is big.) Soy maestra. (I'm a teacher.)
Origen (Origin)	Tú eres de Estados Unidos. (You are from the United States.)
Propiedad (Property)	Él es mi amigo. (He is my friend.) Ella es mi mamá. (She is my mom.)
Fecha de entrega (Deadline)	La tarea es para mañana. (The homework is due tomorrow.)
Ubicación de suceso social (Location of a social event)	La fiesta es en mi casa. (The party is at my house.)
La hora (Time)	Es la una y media. (It's one-thirty.) Son las ocho en punto. (It's eight o'clock.)
Composición (Composition)	La mesa es de madera. (The table is made of wood.)
Frases impersonales (Impersonal phrases)	Es un día bonito. (It's a lovely day.) Es un vestido largo. (It's a long dress.) Es un problema complicado. (It's a complicated problem.)

Here are some useful phrases you can use with *ser*:

Soy (<u>your name</u>). ¿Y tú?	(I'm (<u>your name</u>). And you?)
¿Sos (<u>name of the other person</u>)?	(Are you (<u>name of the other person</u>)?)
Somos estudiantes.	(We are students.)
Sois jóvenes.	(You all are young.)
Ellos son estudiantes.	(They are students.)
¿Ustedes son alumnos?	(Are you all students?)

- To be → *Estar*

In contrast with *ser*, we use *estar* to talk about attributes that are not permanent and are subject to change when we speak about them, whether we talk about them in the past, present, or future. It's an irregular verb, although you will notice that there aren't too many variations in the present tense.

Pronombres (Pronouns)	estar (to be)
yo	estoy
tú	estás
vos	estás
él / ella / usted	está
nosotros / nosotras	estamos
vosotros / vosotras	estáis
ellos / ellas / ustedes	están

Estar can generally refer to the physical location of anything except social events as well as conditions or states. Let's take a look at some examples in a table:

Usage	Examples
Ubicación física de cualquier cosa menos los eventos sociales (Physical location of anything but social events)	El abuelo está en la cocina. (The grandfather is in the kitchen.) El lápiz está en la mesa. (The pencil is on the table.) La familia está en Perú. (The family is in Peru.)
Condición o estado (Condition or state)	Estoy cansado. (I'm tired.) Él está enfermo. (He is sick.) Ella está triste. (She is sad.) Ustedes están felices. (You all are happy.) La pasta está deliciosa. (The pasta is delicious.) Las manzanas están duras. (The apples are hard.)

Why are we using *estar* instead of *ser* to say that a person is tired, sick, sad, or happy? If we were to use *ser*, we would mean that that adjective is actually a permanent characteristic. Even when you know a person who is always tired, they have high energy intervals. To indicate that they are always tired, you will need to say, "*Tú siempre estás cansado,*" *siempre* being "always."

If you were to say, "*Él es enfermo,*" rather than "*Él está enfermo,*" you would be using *enfermo* as a characteristic, meaning that the person you are talking about is, by nature, a sick person. But, then, we wouldn't be talking about their health anymore but their personality, since personality traits don't swing from one extreme to the other as fast as health can.

When we say, "*La pasta está deliciosa,*" we are referring to the food we are currently tasting. This pasta, right here and right now, is delicious. If we said, "*La pasta es deliciosa,*" then we would be describing pasta as a delicious food by nature. The same thing happens when we say, "*Las manzanas son duras,*" rather than, "*Las manzanas están duras.*" If we use *son*, we are saying that all apples are characterized by being hard. If we use *están*, then we are saying that these apples are hard, and we are also leaving room for change. The apples can be hard now, but eventually, they can become softer.

Here are some useful phrases that use *estar*:

Estoy bien. ¿Y usted?	(I'm well. And you?)
Y vos, ¿cómo estás?	(And you (informal), how are you?)
Y usted, ¿cómo está?	(And you (formal), how are you?)
Estamos bien.	(We are well.)
Y vosotras, ¿cómo estáis?	(And you all (females), how are you?)
Y ustedes, ¿cómo están?	(And you all, how are you?)

Adjetivos (Adjectives)

Adjectives are words used to describe nouns. And as such, they need to match the noun in gender and number. Yes, everything revolves around the nouns! We will learn some useful adjectives that will come in handy when you start forming sentences. Remember, we will use these adjectives throughout our lessons, so don't worry if you can't memorize them all right now. Repetition will help you integrate them into your vocabulary.

Complete the table below by writing a sentence with each adjective describing a masculine and feminine person or object.

NOTE: Some adjectives are neutral. Those ending in -e can be applied to both genders.

English	Spanish	Feminine Singular	Masculine Singular
big	grande	La taza es grande. (The cup is big.)	El perro es grande. (The dog is big.)
small	pequeño / chico		
tall	alto		
short (in height)	bajo		
long	largo		
short (in length)	corto		
dark-haired	moreno / morocho		
blonde	rubio		
redheaded	pelirrojo		
cheap	barato		
expensive	caro		
clean	limpio		
dirty	sucio		
easy	fácil		
difficult	difícil		
close	cercano		
far	lejano		
full	lleno		
empty	vacío		
happy	feliz		
sad	triste		
heavy	pesado		
light	ligero / liviano		
good	bueno		
bad	malo		
hot	caliente		
cold	frío		
new	nuevo		
young	joven		
old	viejo		

antique / ancient	antiguo		
poor	pobre		
rich	rico		
fat	gordo		
thin	flaco / delgado		
quick	rápido		
slow	lento		
noisy	ruidoso		
silent	silencioso		
safe	seguro		
dangerous	peligroso		
single	soltero		
married	casado		
hard	duro		
soft / tender	blando		
soft	suave		
strong	fuerte		
weak	débil		
dry	seco		
wet	mojado		
wide	amplio / ancho		
narrow	angosto		
delicious	sabroso / delicioso		
disgusting	repugnante		
intelligent	inteligente / listo		
wise	sabio		
silly	tonto		
kind	amable		
ready	listo		
cute / pretty	bonito / lindo		
ugly	feo		
fun	divertido		
boring	aburrido		

open	abierto		
closed	cerrado		
tired	cansado		
awake	despierto		
crazy	loco		
quiet / peaceful	tranquilo		
sick	enfermo		
healthy	sano		
sweet	dulce		
salty	salado		
fair	justo		
unfair	injusto		
careful	cuidadoso		

How to Form Adverbs

While adjectives describe nouns, adverbs describe verbs. There is a simple formula to form adverbs, which is:

- feminine adjective + -*mente*

Or:

- neutral adjective + -*mente*

Neutral adjectives end in -e, meaning they can be used for masculine or feminine nouns.

The -*mente* suffix that we add to feminine adjectives is the equivalent of the "-lly" added for English adverbs.

Of course, we have a couple of rebels in our rows. "Well" in Spanish is *bien*, while "badly" is *mal*.

Let's do some exercises together, taking some of the adjectives we learned before and turning them into adverbs.

English	Spanish	Spanish Adverb
big / enormous	grande	grandemente
tall / high	alto	
long	largo	
clean	limpio	
dirty	sucio	
easy	fácil	
difficult	difícil	
happy	feliz	
sad	triste	
heavy	pesado	
light	ligero / liviano	
cold	frío	
new	nuevo	
antique	antiguo	
poor	pobre	
rich	rico	
quick	rápido	
slow	lento	
noisy	ruidoso	
silent	silencioso	
safe	seguro	
dangerous	peligroso	
hard	duro	
soft	suave	
strong	fuerte	
weak	débil	
dry	seco	
wide	amplio / ancho	
narrow	angosto	
delicious	delicioso	
disgusting	repugnante	

intelligent	inteligente	
wise	sabio	
silly	tonto	
kind	amable	
ugly	feo	
boring	aburrido	
open	abierto	
tired	cansado	
crazy	loco	
quiet / peaceful	tranquilo	
healthy	sano	
sweet	dulce	
fair	justo	
unfair	injusto	
dangerous	peligroso	
careful	cuidadoso	

How to Use No

To write the negative forms of verbs, you just need to add *no* before the verb. And that's it! Easy peasy, right? Let's see how we place *no* right before verbs:

No hablo español.	(I don't speak Spanish.)
Nosotros no hablamos español.	(We don't speak Spanish.)
No hablo inglés.	(I don't speak English.)
Ella no habla inglés.	(She doesn't speak English.)
No leo bien.	(I don't read well.)
Él no come carne.	(He doesn't eat meat.)
No creo.	(I don't think so.)
No vivo aquí.	(I don't live here.)

How to Form Questions

There are more complex ways to form questions, but we will learn how to do it the simple way. All you have to do is change your intonation, from beginning to end, to turn an otherwise affirmative statement into a question.

¿Ellos no hablan español?	(They don't speak Spanish?)
¿Ellas no hablan inglés?	(They (all females) don't speak English?)
¿Ustedes no viven aquí?	(You (all) don't live here?)
¿Tú hablas inglés?	(Do you (informal) speak English?)
¿Usted lee español?	(Do you (formal) read Spanish?)
¿Vosotros coméis carne?	(Do you (all) eat meat?)

How to Use Question Words

We can make our questions more complex by adding question words. It's not hard to do; it just requires a little practice. We will go through each question word and look at some examples:

¿Quién? (Who?)

- *Quién* is a useful pronoun meaning "who" or "whom." *Quién* goes in front of the verb. If you want, the pronoun can also be included. If you do, the pronoun goes after the verb.

¿Quién eres tú?	(Who are you?)
¿Quiénes son ellos?	(Who are they?)
¿Quién es el profesor?	(Who is the teacher?)
¿Quién está en la casa?	(Who is in the house?)
¿Quiénes estudian español?	(Who studies Spanish?)

¿Qué? (What?)

- When we use *Qué* + *ser* + noun in a question, we are asking about the actual meaning of a noun. You can use this structure to ask for the meaning of any word.

  ¿Qué es "mesa"?   (What is "table"?)

- When we use *Qué* + verb in a question, we are asking about the object associated with that verb. This time, I will show examples where we omit mentioning the pronoun:

¿Qué comes (tú)?	(What do you eat?)
¿Qué quieren (ellos)?	(What do they want?)
¿Qué lee (usted)?	(What do you read?)
¿Qué mira (ella)?	(What does she look at?)

¿Cuál? (Which?)

- We use *Cuál* to ask questions where you have many options and need to pick one. It also uses a very specific structure: *Cuál* + *es* + noun.

  ¿Cuál es el número de teléfono?   (What is the phone number?)

- Notice that, even though you use "What" in English, we use *Cuál* in Spanish because there are several options, and you have to select one.

¿Cuál es el hospedaje?	(Which lodging is it?)
¿Cuál es la contraseña del wifi?	(What is the wifi password?)

¿Cuánto? (How much? / How many?)

- We use *Cuánto* to ask about quantity. Depending on the gender and number of the noun, this question word will be *cuánto*, *cuánta*, *cuántos* or *cuántas*.

¿Cuánto dinero necesito?	(How much money do I need?)
¿Cuánto cuesta?	(How much does it cost?)
¿Cuántos amigos tienes?	(How many friends do you have?)
¿Cuántas hermanas son?	(How many sisters are you all?)

¿Cómo? (How?)

- We use Cómo to ask about the way something is done.

¿Cómo vamos al parque?	(How are we going to the park?)
¿Cómo haces ejercicio?	(How do you work out?)
¿Cómo estudias español?	(How do you study Spanish?)
¿Cómo se dice...?	(How do you say...?)

¿Cuándo? (When?)

- We use Cuándo to ask when an event happened, happens, or will happen.

¿Cuándo viajas?	(When do you travel?)
¿Cuándo almozarmos?	(When do we have lunch?)
¿Cuándo regresan (ustedes)?	(When do you all come back?)

¿Dónde? (Where?)

- We use Dónde to ask about the location of an event, person, animal, thing, etc.

¿Dónde está el lápiz?	(Where is the pencil?)
¿Dónde es la fiesta?	(Where is the party?)
¿Dónde está tu amigo?	(Where is your friend?)
¿Dónde es la reunión?	(Where is the meeting?)

¿*Adónde*? (To where?)

– We use Adónde to ask for the destination of a person.

¿Adónde viajas?	(Where are you traveling to?)
¿Adónde vamos?	(Where are we going?)

¿*De dónde*? (From where?)

– We use De dónde to ask about the place something comes from.

¿De dónde vienes?	(Where are you coming from?)
¿De dónde salió la ardilla?	(Where did the squirrel come from?)

¿*Por qué*? (Why?)

– We use Por qué to ask about the direct cause of something. Note that in responding with the term "because," the words por and que come together to form a compound word.

¿Por qué estudias español?	(Why do you study Spanish?)
Estudio español porque mi mamá es de México.	(I study Spanish, because my mom is from Mexico.)
¿Por qué estáis en el parque?	(Why are you all at the park?)
Estamos en el parque porque es bonito.	(We are at the park because it's pretty.)
¿Por qué quiere el papel?	(Why does he want the paper?)
Él quiere el papel porque es azul.	(He wants the paper, because it is blue.)

¿*Para qué*? (For what?)

– We use Para qué to ask about the purpose of something.

¿Para qué estudias español?	(What do you study Spanish for?)
Estudio español para hablar con mi familia mexicana.	(I study Spanish to talk with my Mexican family.)

¿Para qué estáis en el parque? (What are you at the park for?)
Estamos en el parque para jugar. (We are at the park to play.)

¿Para qué quiere el papel? (What does he want the paper for?)
Él quiere el papel para dibujar. (He wants the paper to draw.)

- Here's another helpful table to organize the information.

Spanish	English
¿Quién?	Who?
¿Qué?	What?
¿Cuál?	Which?
¿Cuánto? / ¿Cuántos?	How much? / How many?
¿Cómo?	How?
¿Cuándo?	When?
¿Dónde?	Where?
¿Adónde?	To where?
¿De dónde?	From where?
¿Por qué?	Why?
¿Para qué?	For what?

TAREA

HOMEWORK

Dear reader and student, I will give you some critical advice. Doing this will assist you in making significant progress in your language journey. So pay attention, because here it is:

Practice.

Yes, as simple (and sometimes, as hard) as it is, practice. When I say practice, I don't mean that you must study for hours every day. Some people can do it, but we all have different lives and learning styles. Do what works best for you, but do it consistently.

In this early stage, so close to the starting point, it is essential to exercise your memory. One way to build consistency is habit stacking. Pair your new studying habits with habits you have already successfully incorporated into your daily routine.

Do you enjoy a cup of coffee every morning while watching the news? Maybe you can listen to the news in Spanish and turn on the Spanish subtitles. Your unconscious mind can help you unlock many bonuses. Exposing it to Spanish will help you get used to the accent and include new words into your active vocabulary. You will also learn how to pronounce words correctly while training your ear.

If you want to exercise your mind consciously, you can spend at least fifteen minutes a day watching a show or a movie in Spanish, preferably with Spanish subtitles. Keep a notebook next to you, so you can record new words or phrases you may want to use later. You can also re-watch your favorite movie or show in Spanish. Using Spanish subtitles will help you focus more on your target language and help you learn the spelling of new words you hear.

Spice up your playlist with Spanish music! There are so many genres you will love. From salsa and cumbias to rap and boleros. Is there a country you want to visit in particular? Become acquainted with the culture through music. Listen to a local Spanish language radio station or an online station. To enrich the experience, search for the lyrics and try to follow them as the music plays. I have a running YouTube playlist featuring artists from all of the Spanish-speaking countries. You can access this from lafelizbooks.com. Check out the *¡Viva viernes!* section to learn more about songs that are featured on Fridays.

Another thing you can do to improve your conversational skills is practice different ways to introduce yourself and share information about your life. You can start by learning how to say your name in Spanish. Many English names have a Spanish equivalent—for example, George translates to *Jorge*.

Don't miss the opportunity to practice Spanish with a native speaker. Yes, yes, I know, it can be scary... but only in the beginning! Once you get the ball rolling, developing your conversational skills will become easier. So take advantage of the opportunities life gives you to improve.

Practice, even if it is challenging in the beginning. Do something today that your future self will thank you for.

Leave a
1-Click Review!

It is my sincere wish to help others feel confident and excited about speaking Spanish. Therefore, if you think that I have accomplished my goal, please leave an honest review on the link below. By leaving a review, you will help make my book more visible to other potential Spanish learners.

SUMMARY

It's time to pause and take stock of what you have learned so far! We started First Period not knowing how to read in Spanish... and now you can hold a basic conversation! We took a deep dive into pronunciation by checking accents and how to separate words into syllables. And you learned the number one rule to PERFECT your spoken Spanish: keeping the sounds of the vowels short and dry.

You are now able to distinguish cognates from false cognates—those shady little fellows that have the potential to cause laughs and embarrassment. Remember that everything needs to match in Spanish. Every noun has a gender and can be singular or plural. Definite and indefinite articles, as well as adjectives, have to match them.

Together, we learned many phrases to be able to engage in a short conversation and make simple statements. Then, we added pronouns and the most useful and common verbs to our vocabulary. Finally, we hit a significant milestone when we learned to conjugate regular verbs in the present tense and to use *ser* and *estar*. We complemented that knowledge by understanding how to use interrogative or question words.

And let's not forget all the words we reviewed to expand your vocabulary. Put everything you have learned into practice because, without a doubt, now you can speak Spanish. *First Period: Language Arts* ends here. *La primera hora: Lenguaje y comunicación* termina aquí... but class is not dismissed yet! *Second Period: Math* starts soon! Grab a pencil and paper, keep your mind sharp, and get ready for *La segunda hora: Matemáticas.*

In my second book, *Volume 2: Math*, we will tap into cardinal and ordinal numbers, express time and dates, talk about measures and temperature, use quantitative adjectives, and learn many verbs and phrases you will be able to use to carry on more complex conversations. See you in class!

Audiobook Coming Soon!

An audiobook version of

YOU CAN SPEAK SPANISH! - VOLUME 1

is coming soon. If you want to be one of the first people

to know when it's released AND receive a **FREE** copy,

sign up at **http://lafelizbooks.com/contact/**

REFERENCES

Fernández-Dobao, A., & Herschensohn, J. (2020). Present tense verb morphology of Spanish HL and L2 children in dual immersion: Feature Reassembly revisited. *Linguistic Approaches to Bilingualism*, 10(6), 775-804.

Herbert Turk, L. (1946). *Así se aprende el español*. Lexington: D. C. Heath & Company.

Kattán-Ibarra, J., & Wilkie, I. (2004). *Modern Spanish Grammar Workbook*. New York: Routledge.

Kendris, C., & Kendris, T. (2019). *Pocket Spanish Grammar*. New York: Barrons Educational Series.

Montemayor, R. D., & Escobar Hernández, O. (2010). *Aprende español ahora: nivel intermedio A 1* (Publication No. 194134856) [Doctoral dissertation, Universidad de Panamá]. Vicerrectoría de Investigación y Postgrado.

Nissenberg, G. (2016). *Practice Makes Perfect Complete Spanish Grammar*. New York: McGraw Hill.

Prado, M. (1997). *Advanced Spanish grammar: a self-teaching guide*. New York: John Wiley & Sons, Inc.

Rini, J. (2019). Changing Genders: Linguistic Factors Beyond Ambiguous Gender Marking and the Case of Spanish *el arte vs el ave and el hambre*. *Bulletin of Spanish Studies*, 96(1), 1-16.

Roca, I. (2019). Spanish verb and non-verb stress. In S. Colina & F. Martínez-Gil (Eds.), *The Routledge Handbook of Spanish Phonology* (1st ed., pp. 181-221). Routledge.

Rodriguez, S., & Carretero, J. (1996). A Formal Approach to Spanish Grammar: the COES Tools. *Procesamiento del Lenguaje Natural*, 19.

GLOSARIO (GLOSSARY)

Glossary Key

Abbreviation	Meaning
adj	adjective
adv	adverb
art	article
con	conjunction
f	feminine noun
m	masculine noun
prep	preposition
pro	pronoun
v	verb

Spanish to English

Spanish	Grammar	English
A		
abierto	*adj*	open
abogado	*m*	lawyer
abrazo	*m*	hug
abril	*m*	April
abuelo	*m*	grandfather
aburrido	*adj*	boring
Adiós	*m*	Goodbye!
adjetivo	*m*	adjective
adónde	*adv*	to where
aéreo	*adj*	aerial
aeropuerto	*m*	airport
agua	*f*	water
ahorros	*m*	savings
aire	*m*	air
ajonjolí	*m*	sesame
albahaca	*f*	basil
alcohol	*m*	alcohol
alegría	*f*	joy
alergia	*f*	allergy
alfabeto	*m*	alphabet
algo	*pro*	something
alma	*f*	soul
almorzar	*v*	to have lunch
alta / alto	*adj*	tall
altavoz	*m*	speaker
alumna	*f*	female student
alumno	*m*	male student
amable	*adj*	kind
amar	*v*	to love
amigo	*m*	friend

amo	v	I love
amplio	adj	wide
ancho	adj	wide
angosto	adj	narrow
año	m	year
anteojos	m	glasses
antes	prep	before
antiguo	adj	antique / ancient
antiinflamatorio	m / adj	anti-inflammatory
aplicación	f	app
aprender	v	to learn
aquí	adv	here
árbol	m	tree
ardilla	f	squirrel
artículos	m	articles
Asia	f	Asia
ataúd	m	coffin
ateo	m / adj	atheist
ático	m	attic
aula	f	classroom
aún	adv	still
auto	m	car
autor	m	author
avergonzado	adj	embarrassed
avión	m	plane
azahar	m	orange blossom
B		
baile	m	dance
bajo	adj	short (in height)
banco	m	bank
baño	m	bathroom
barato	adj	cheap
beber	v	to drink
biblioteca	f	library

bien	*adv*	well
bienestar	*m*	well-being
biología	*f*	biology
blando	*adj*	soft / tender
bolígrafo	*m*	pen
bonito	*adj*	beautiful / cute / lovely / pretty
borrador	*m*	eraser
Brasil	*m*	Brazil
buena / bueno	*adj*	good
Buenas		Hi
Buenas noches		Good night
Buenas tardes		Good afternoon
Buenos días		Good morning
búho	*m*	owl
C		
cabeza	*f*	head
cacao	*m*	cocoa
cacatúa	*f*	cockatoo
café	*m*	coffee
caliente	*adj*	hot
calle	*f*	street
cámara	*f*	camera
camión	*m*	truck
canción	*f*	song
canoa	*f*	canoe
cansado	*adj*	tired
capitalismo	*m*	capitalism
característica	*f*	characteristic
carne	*f*	meat
caro	*adj*	expensive
carro	*m*	car / cart
carta	*f*	letter / menu
casa	*f*	house
casado	*adj*	married

cercano	adj	close
cerrado	adj	closed
césped	m	grass / lawn
Chao		bye
chico	adj	small
chocolate	m / adj	chocolate
chofer	m / f	driver
cien	m / adj	one hundred
ciudad	f	city
clase	f	class
coche	m	car
cocina	f	kitchen
coeficiente	m	coefficient
cognado	m	cognate
colegio	m	school
color	m	color
comedor	m	dining room
comer	v	to eat
cometa	m	comet
cómo	adv	how
compartir	v	to share
complicado	adj	complicated
composición	f	composition
computadora	f	computer
con	prep	with
condición	f	condition
construir	v	to build
contigo	pro	with you (informal)
continuar	v	to continue
contraseña	f	password
cooperar	v	to cooperate
correctamente	adv	correctly
correr	v	to run
corto	adj	short (in length)

cosa	*f*	thing
costumbre	*f*	custom
creer	*v*	to believe
cuaderno	*m*	notebook
cuál	*pro*	which / what
cualquier	*pro*	any
cuándo	*adv*	when
cuánto / cuánta / cuántos / cuántas	*adj*	how much / how many
cuarto	*m*	bedroom / room
cuatro	*m / adj*	four
cuidadoso	*adj*	careful
cumpleaños	*m*	birthday
cuota	*f*	fee
D		
de	*prep*	from / of
de dónde	*adv*	from where
débil	*adj*	weak
decirse	*v*	to be said
delgado	*adj*	thin
deliciosa / delicioso	*adj*	delicious
deseo	*m*	wish
despedida	*f*	goodbye
despedirse	*v*	to say goodbye
despierto	*adj*	awake
día	*m*	day
dibujar	*v*	to draw
diccionario	*m*	dictionary
dice	*v*	say / says
dientes	*m*	teeth
diez	*m / adj*	ten
difícil	*adj*	difficult
dinero	*m*	money
diptongo	*m*	diphthong

director	*m*	director / principal
directora	*f*	director / principal
divertido	*adj*	fun
dominó	*m*	domino
dónde	*adv*	where
dormitorio	*m*	bedroom
dos	*m / adj*	two
dulce	*adj*	sweet
dura / duro	*m / adj*	hard
E		
ecológico	*adj*	ecological
ejemplo	*m*	example
ejercicio	*m*	exercise
el	*art*	the
él	*pro*	he
ella	*pro*	she
ellas	*pro*	they (female)
ellos	*pro*	they (all-male or mixed group)
email	*m*	email
embarazada	*adj*	pregnant
empleado	*m*	employee
en	*prep*	in
encantada / encantado	*adj*	nice to meet you
enfermo	*adj*	sick
engrapadora	*f*	stapler
enlace	*m*	link
ensalada	*f*	salad
enseñar	*v*	to teach
entrada	*f*	entrance
equipo	*m*	team
escribir	*v*	to write
escritor	*m*	writer
escritora	*f*	writer
escuela	*f*	school

español	*m / adj*	Spanish
esposo	*m*	husband
estado	*m*	state
Estados Unidos	*m*	United States
estadounidense	*adj*	American (U.S.)
estar	*v*	to be
estudiante	*m / f*	student
estudiar	*v*	to study
estudio	*v*	I study
euro	*m*	euro
evento	*m*	event
examen	*m*	exam
excitado	*adj*	aroused / stimulated
explorar	*v*	to explore
F		
fácil	*adj*	easy
falso	*adj*	false
familia	*f*	family
favorito	*adj*	favorite
fecha de entrega	*f*	deadline
felicidad	*f*	happiness
felicitaciones	*f*	congratulations
feliz	*adj*	happy
feo	*adj*	ugly
ficticio	*adj*	fictitious
fiesta	*f*	party
final	*m*	end
físico	*adj*	physical
flaco	*adj*	thin
flor	*f*	flower
flúor	*m*	flouride
forma	*f*	shape
foto	*f*	photo
fotografía	*f*	photograph

frase impersonal	*f*	impersonal phrase
fríen	*v*	they / you all fry
frío	*adj*	cold
fuerte	*adj*	strong

G

gafas	*f*	glasses
ganar	*v*	to win
garaje	*m*	garage
género	*m*	gender
gimnasio	*m*	gym / gymnasium
globo	*m*	globe / balloon
goma de borrar	*f*	eraser
gordo	*adj*	fat
gracias	*f*	thank you
gramática	*f*	grammar
grande	*adj*	big
grandemente	*adv*	enormously
grapadora	*f*	stapler
grúa	*f*	crane
guapo	*adj*	handsome
gusto	*m*	pleasure

H

haber	*v*	there is / there are
habitación	*f*	bedroom / room
hablar	*v*	to speak
hacer	*v*	to do
hacha	*f*	ax
hasta	*prep*	until
hay	*v*	there is / there are
hermana	*f*	sister
hiato	*m*	hiatus
hijo	*m*	son / child
hilo	*m*	thread
hindúes	*m / f*	Hindus

historia	f	history / story
hola		hello
hombre	m	man
hora	f	time
horario	m	schedule
hospedaje	m	lodging
hoy	adv	today
I		
idioma	m	language
iglúes	m	igloos
igualmente	adv	likewise / equally
impresora	f	printer
increíble	adj	incredible
infinitivo	m	infinitive
inglés	m / adj	English
injusto	adj	unfair
instinto	m	instinct
instrucción	f	instruction
instrumento	m	instrument
inteligente	adj	intelligent
interesante	adj	interesting
J		
jardín	m	garden
joven	adj	young
judío	m / adj	Jewish
juego	m	game
jugar	v	to play
jugo	m	juice
juicio	m	judgment
justo	adj	fair
K		
kilo	m	kilo
L		
la	art	the

labor	f	labor
lápiz	m	pencil
largo	adj	long
las	art	the
lección	f	lesson
lector	m	reader
leer	v	to read
legumbre	f	legume
lejano	adj	far
lenguaje y comunicación	m	language arts
lentamente	adv	slowly
lentes	m	glasses
lento	adj	slow
ley	f	law
libro	m	book
ligero	adj	light
limón	m	lemon
limpio	adj	clean
lindo	adj	cute / pretty
listo	adj	intelligent / ready
liviano	adj	light
llamarse	v	to call oneself
llave	f	key
lleno	adj	full
lo siento		I'm sorry
loco	adj	crazy
los	art	the
luz	f	light
M		
madera	f	wood
maestra	f	teacher
maestro	m	teacher
maíz	m	corn
mal	adv	badly

malo	*adj*	bad
mamá	*f*	mom
mañana	*adv*	tomorrow
mano	*f*	hand
manzana	*f*	apple
mapa	*m*	map
mar	*m*	sea
marea	*f*	tide
masculino	*adj*	masculine
matemáticas	*f*	mathematics
memoria	*f*	memory
menos	*prep*	except
mensaje de texto	*m*	text message
menú	*m*	menu
mesa	*f*	table
mi	*adj*	my
micrófono	*m*	microphone
miel	*f*	honey
mil	*m / adj*	one thousand
mío	*adj*	mine
mirar	*v*	to look / to watch
mochila	*f*	backpack
mojado	*adj*	wet
moreno	*adj*	dark-haired
morocho	*adj*	dark-haired
morral	*m*	satchel
mucho	*adj*	a lot
mucho gusto		nice to meet you
mujer	*f*	woman
mutuo	*adj*	mutual
muy	*adv*	very
muy bien	*adv*	very well
N		
necesitar	*v*	to need

necesito	v	I need
niña	f	girl
niño	m	boy
no	adv	no / not
nombre	m	name
nosotras	pro	we (female)
nosotros	pro	we (all-male or mixed group)
noúmeno	m	noumenon
nueve	m / adj	nine
nuevo	adj	new
nuez	f	nut
número	m	number
Ñ		
ñame	m	yam
O		
ocho	m / adj	eight
oficina	f	office
oigo	v	I hear
oír	v	to hear
ola	f	wave
olor	m	smell
oportunidad	f	opportunity
ordenador	m	computer
origen	m	origin
P		
pagar	v	to pay
página	f	page
país	m	country
pantalla	f	screen
pantalones	m	pants
papá	m	dad
papel	m	paper
para	prep	for / to
para qué	con	for what

pared	*f*	wall
parque	*m*	park
pasillo	*m*	hallway
pasta	*f*	pasta
patio	*m*	patio
paz	*f*	peace
pedir	*v*	to ask for
pegamento	*m*	glue
película	*f*	movie
peligro	*m*	danger
peligroso	*adj*	dangerous
pelirrojo	*adj*	redheaded
pequeño	*adj*	small
período	*m*	period
persona	*f*	person
persuadir	*v*	to persuade
Perú	*m*	Peru
peruana / peruano	*adj*	Peruvian
pesado	*adj*	heavy
pez	*m*	fish
piel	*f*	skin
piso	*m*	floor
pizarra	*f*	board
placer	*m*	pleasure
pobre	*adj*	poor
poema	*m*	poem
por	*prep*	for / by
por qué	*adv*	why
porche	*m*	porch
portátil	*m*	laptop
portugués	*m / adj*	Portuguese
preferido	*adj*	favorite
preparar	*v*	to prepare
presentarse	*v*	to introduce oneself

presente indicativo	*m*	present indicative
primaria	*f*	primary school
primero / primera	*adj*	first
problema	*m*	problem
profesor	*m*	professor / teacher
profesora	*f*	professor / teacher
pronombres	*m*	pronouns
pronto	*adv*	soon
propiedad	*f*	property
próxima / próximo	*adj*	next
pueblo	*m*	town / village
puerta	*f*	door
pupitre	*m*	school desk
Q		
qué	*pro / adj*	what
querer	*v*	to want
quién / quiénes	*pro*	who
quiero	*v*	I want
química	*f*	chemistry
R		
radio	*f*	radio
rápidamente	*adv*	quickly
rápido	*adj*	fast / quick
ratón	*m*	computer mouse
razón	*f*	reason
recibir	*v*	to receive
red	*f*	internet / net
regla	*f*	ruler
regresar	*v*	to return
reír	*v*	to laugh
reloj	*m*	clock
repugnante	*adj*	disgusting
restaurante	*m*	restaurant
reunión	*f*	meeting

reunir	v	to gather / meet
rey	m	king
rico	adj	rich
ríes	v	you laugh
río	m	river
roído	adj	gnawed
rompecabezas	m	puzzle
rubio	adj	blonde
ruido	m	noise
ruidoso	adj	noisy
rumor	m	rumor
S		
sabio	adj	wise
sabroso	adj	delicious
sacapuntas	m	pencil sharpener
sala	f	living room
salado	adj	salty
salir	v	to go out / to come out
sano	adj	healthy
sé	v	I know
seco	adj	dry
secundaria	f	middle school / high school
segundo	adj	second
seguro	adj	safe
seis	m / adj	six
ser	v	to be
Seúl	f	Seoul
si	con	if
sí	adv	yes
siempre	adv	always
siete	m / adj	seven
silencioso	adj	silent
silla	f	chair
social	adj	social

sofá	*m*	sofa
sol	*m*	sun
soledad	*f*	loneliness
soltero	*adj*	single
sorpresa	*f*	surprise
sótano	*m*	basement
soy	*v*	I am
suave	*adj*	soft
suceso	*m*	event
sucio	*adj*	dirty
sueño	*m*	dream
sustantivo	*m*	noun
T		
tan	*adv*	so
tarea	*f*	homework / task
taza	*f*	cup
té	*m*	tea
teatro	*m*	theater
techo	*m*	ceiling / roof
teclado	*m*	keyboard
televisión	*f*	television
televisor	*m*	television
tema	*m*	theme / song
tener	*v*	to have
tengo	*v*	I have
terminación	*f*	ending
terraza	*f*	terrace / balcony
tienes	*v*	you (informal) have
tijeras	*f*	scissors
toalla	*f*	towel
tonto	*adj*	silly
traer	*v*	to bring
tranquilo	*adj*	quiet / peaceful
transeúnte	*m / f*	passerby

transplante	m	transplant
triptongo	m	triphthong
triste	adj	sad
tu	adj	your (informal)
tú	pro	you (informal)

U

ubicación	f	location
un	art	a / an
una	art	a / an
unas	art	some
uniforme	m	uniform
universidad	f	university
unos	art	some
Uruguay	m	Uruguay
usted	pro	you (formal)
ustedes	pro	you (plural)
usuario	m	user

V

vacación	f	vacation
vacío	adj	empty
vamos	v	we go
velocidad	f	speed
venir	v	to come
ventana	f	window
ventilador de techo	m	ceiling fan
ver	v	to see
verbo	m	verb
vestido	m	dress
vez	f	time
viajar	v	to travel
viejo	adj	old
vienes	v	you (informal) come
viento	m	wind
violeta	f	violet

viuda	*f*	widow
vivir	*v*	to live
volumen	*m*	volume
vos	*pro*	you (informal)
vosotras	*pro*	you (informal plural - female)
vosotros	*pro*	you (informal plural - all male or mixed group)
voz	*f*	voice
W		
wifi	*m*	wifi
X		
xilófono	*m*	xylophone
Y		
y	*con*	and
yo	*pro*	I
yoga	*m*	yoga
Z		
zapatos	*m*	shoes
zoo	*m*	zoo

English to Spanish

English	Spanish
A	
a / an	un / una
a lot	mucho
adjective	adjetivo
aerial	aéreo
air	aire
airport	aeropuerto
alcohol	alcohol
allergy	alergia
alphabet	alfabeto
always	siempre
American (U.S.)	estadounidense
and	y
anti-inflammatory	antiinflamatorio
antique / ancient	antiguo
any	cualquier
app	aplicación
apple	manzana
April	abril
aroused / stimulated	excitado
articles	artículos
Asia	Asia
(to) ask for	pedir
atheist	ateo
attic	ático
author	autor
awake	despierto
ax	hacha
B	
backpack	mochila
bad	malo

badly	mal
balcony	terraza
balloon	globo
bank	banco
basement	sótano
basil	albahaca
bathroom	baño
(to) be	estar / ser
beautiful	bonito
bedroom	dormitorio / cuarto / habitación
before	antes
(to) believe	creer
big	grande
biology	biología
birthday	cumpleaños
blonde	rubio
board	pizarra
book	libro
boring	aburrido
boy	niño
Brazil	Brasil
(to) bring	traer
(to) build	construir
by	por
bye	Chao
C	
(to) call oneself	llamarse
camera	cámara
canoe	canoa
capitalism	capitalismo
car	auto / carro / coche
careful	cuidadoso
cart	carro
ceiling	techo

ceiling fan	ventilador de techo
chair	silla
characteristic	característica
cheap	barato
chemistry	química
child	hijo
chocolate	chocolate
city	ciudad
class	clase
classroom	aula
clean	limpio
clock	reloj
close	cercano
closed	cerrado
cockatoo	cacatúa
cocoa	cacao
coefficient	coeficiente
coffee	café
coffin	ataúd
cognate	cognado
cold	frío
color	color
(to) come	venir
(to) come out	salir
comet	cometa
complicated	complicado
composition	composición
computer	computadora / ordenador
computer mouse	ratón
condition	condición
congratulations	felicitaciones
(to) continue	continuar
(to) cooperate	cooperar
corn	maíz

correctly	correctamente
country	país
crane	grúa
crazy	loco
cup	taza
custom	costumbre
cute	bonito / lindo
D	
dad	papá
dance	baile
danger	peligro
dangerous	peligroso
dark-haired	moreno / morocho
day	día
deadline	fecha de entrega
delicious	delicioso / sabroso
dictionary	diccionario
difficult	difícil
dining room	comedor
diphthong	diptongo
director / principal	director / directora
dirty	sucio
disgusting	repugnante
(to) do	hacer
domino	dominó
door	puerta
(to) draw	dibujar
dream	sueño
dress	vestido
(to) drink	beber
driver	chofer
dry	seco
E	
easy	fácil

(to) eat	comer
ecological	ecológico
eight	ocho
email	email
embarrassed	avergonzado
employee	empleado
empty	vacío
end	final
ending	terminación
English	inglés
enormously	grandemente
entrance	entrada
equally	igualmente
eraser	borrador / goma de borrar
euro	euro
event	evento / suceso
exam	examen
example	ejemplo
except	menos
exercise	ejercicio
expensive	caro
(to) explore	explorar
F	
fair	justo
false	falso
family	familia
far	lejano
fast / quick	rápido
fat	gordo
favorite	favorito / preferido
fee	cuota
fictitious	ficticio
first	primero / primera
fish	pez

floor	piso
flouride	flúor
flower	flor
for	para / por
for what	para qué
four	cuatro
friend	amigo
from	de
from where	de dónde
full	lleno
fun	divertido
G	
game	juego
garage	garaje
garden	jardín
(to) gather	reunir
gender	género
girl	niña
glasses	anteojos / gafas / lentes
globe	globo
glue	pegamento
gnawed	roído
(to) go out	salir
good	buena / bueno
Good afternoon	Buenas tardes
Good morning	Buenos días
Good night	Buenas noches
goodbye	despedida
Goodbye!	Adiós
(to say) goodbye	despedirse
grammar	gramática
grandfather	abuelo
grass	césped
gym / gymnasium	gimnasio

H	
hallway	pasillo
hand	mano
handsome	guapo
happiness	felicidad
happy	feliz
hard	dura / duro
(to) have	tener
he	él
head	cabeza
healthy	sano
(to) hear	oír
heavy	pesado
hello	hola
here	aquí
Hi	Buenas
hiatus	hiato
high school	secundaria
Hindus	hindúes
history / story	historia
homework / task	tarea
honey	miel
hot	caliente
house	casa
how	cómo
how much / how many	cuánto / cuánta / cuántos / cuántas
hug	abrazo
husband	esposo
I	
I	yo
I am	soy
I have	tengo
I hear	oigo
I know	sé

I love	amo
I need	necesito
I study	estudio
I want	quiero
I'm sorry	lo siento
if	si
igloo	iglú
impersonal phrase	frase impersonal
in	en
incredible	increíble
infinitive	infinitivo
instinct	instinto
instruction	instrucción
instrument	instrumento
intelligent	inteligente / listo
interesting	interesante
internet	red
(to) introduce oneself	presentarse
J	
Jewish	judío
joy	alegría
judgment	juicio
juice	jugo
K	
key	llave
keyboard	teclado
kilo	kilo
kind	amable
king	rey
kitchen	cocina
L	
labor	labor
language	idioma
language arts	lenguaje y comunicación

laptop	portátil
(to) laugh	reír
law	ley
lawn	césped
lawyer	abogado
(to) learn	aprender
legume	legumbre
lemon	limón
lesson	lección
letter	carta
library	biblioteca
light (adjective)	ligero / liviano
light (noun)	luz
likewise	igualmente
link	enlace
(to) live	vivir
living room	sala
location	ubicación
lodging	hospedaje
loneliness	soledad
long	largo
(to) look	mirar
(to) love	amar
lovely	bonito
(to have) lunch	almorzar
M	
man	hombre
map	mapa
married	casado
masculine	masculino
mathematics	matemáticas
meat	carne
(to) meet	reunir
meeting	reunión

memory	memoria
menu	carta / menú
microphone	micrófono
middle school	secundaria
mine	mío
mom	mamá
money	dinero
movie	película
mutual	mutuo
my	mi
N	
name	nombre
narrow	angosto
(to) need	necesitar
net	red
new	nuevo
next	próxima / próximo
nice to meet you	encantada / encantado / mucho gusto
nine	nueve
no	no
noise	ruido
noisy	ruidoso
not	no
notebook	cuaderno
noumenon	noúmeno
noun	sustantivo
number	número
nut	nuez
O	
of	de
office	oficina
old	viejo
one hundred	cien
one thousand	mil

open	abierto
opportunity	oportunidad
orange blossom	azahar
origin	origen
owl	búho
P	
page	página
pants	pantalones
paper	papel
park	parque
party	fiesta
passerby	transeúnte
password	contraseña
pasta	pasta
patio	patio
(to) pay	pagar
peace	paz
peaceful	tranquilo
pen	bolígrafo
pencil	lápiz
pencil sharpener	sacapuntas
period	período
person	persona
(to) persuade	persuadir
Peru	Perú
Peruvian	peruana / peruano
photo	foto
photograph	fotografía
physical	físico
plane	avión
(to) play	jugar
pleasure	gusto / placer
poem	poema
poor	pobre

porch	porche
Portuguese	portugués
pregnant	embarazada
prepare	preparar
present indicative	presente indicativo
pretty	bonito / lindo
primary school	primaria
printer	impresora
problem	problema
professor / teacher	profesor / profesora
pronouns	pronombres
property	propiedad
puzzle	rompecabezas
Q	
quickly	rápidamente
quiet	tranquilo
R	
radio	radio
(to) read	leer
reader	lector
ready	listo
reason	razón
(to) receive	recibir
redheaded	pelirrojo
restaurant	restaurante
(to) return	regresar
rich	rico
river	río
roof	techo
room	cuarto / habitación
ruler	regla
rumor	rumor
(to) run	correr
S	

sad	triste
safe	seguro
(to be) said	decirse
salad	ensalada
salty	salado
satchel	morral
savings	ahorros
say / says	dice
schedule	horario
school	colegio / escuela
school desk	pupitre
scissors	tijeras
screen	pantalla
sea	mar
second	segundo
(to) see	ver
Seoul	Seúl
sesame	ajonjolí
seven	siete
shape	forma
(to) share	compartir
she	ella
shoes	zapatos
short (in height)	bajo
short (in length)	corto
sick	enfermo
silent	silencioso
silly	tonto
single	soltero
sister	hermana
six	seis
skin	piel
slow	lento
slowly	lentamente

small	chico / pequeño
smell	olor
so	tan
social	social
sofa	sofá
soft (smooth)	suave
soft (tender)	blando
some	unas / unos
something	algo
son	hijo
song	canción
song	tema
soon	pronto
soul	alma
Spanish	español
(to) speak	hablar
speaker	altavoz
speed	velocidad
squirrel	ardilla
stapler	engrapadora / grapadora
state	estado
still	aún
street	calle
strong	fuerte
student	alumna / alumno / estudiante
(to) study	estudiar
sun	sol
surprise	sorpresa
sweet	dulce
T	
table	mesa
tall	alta / alto
tea	té
(to) teach	enseñar

teacher	maestra / maestro
team	equipo
teeth	dientes
television	televisión / televisor
ten	diez
terrace	terraza
text message	mensaje de texto
thank you	gracias
the	el / la / las / los
theater	teatro
theme	tema
there is / there are	haber / hay
they (all-male or mixed group)	ellos
they (female)	ellas
thin	delgado / flaco
thing	cosa
thread	hilo
tide	marea
time (one time)	vez
time (telling time)	hora
tired	cansado
to (in order to)	para
today	hoy
tomorrow	mañana
towel	toalla
town	pueblo
transplant	transplante
(to) travel	viajar
tree	árbol
triphthong	triptongo
truck	camión
two	dos
U	
ugly	feo

unfair	injusto
uniform	uniforme
United States	Estados Unidos
university	universidad
until	hasta
Uruguay	Uruguay
user	usuario
V	
vacation	vacación
verb	verbo
very	muy
very well	muy bien
village	pueblo
violet	violeta
voice	voz
volume	volumen
W	
wall	pared
(to) want	querer
(to) watch	mirar
water	agua
wave	ola
we (all male or mixed group)	nosotros
we (female)	nosotras
we go	vamos
weak	débil
well	bien
well-being	bienestar
wet	mojado
what	qué / cuál
when	cuándo
where	dónde
where to	adónde
which	cuál

who	quién / quiénes
why	por qué
wide	amplio
wide	ancho
widow	viuda
wifi	wifi
(to) win	ganar
wind	viento
window	ventana
wise	sabio
wish	deseo
with	con
with you (informal)	contigo
woman	mujer
wood	madera
(to) write	escribir
writer	escritor / escritora
X	
xylophone	xilófono
Y	
yam	ñame
year	año
yes	sí
yoga	yoga
you (formal)	usted
you (informal plural – all-male or mixed group)	vosotros
you (informal plural - female)	vosotras
you (informal)	tú / vos
you (plural)	ustedes
young	joven
your (informal)	tu
Z	
zoo	zoo

RESPUESTAS (ANSWERS)

Syllable Practice

Palabra (Word)	Significado (Meaning)	Sílabas (Syllables)
voz	voice	voz (1 syllable)
limón	lemon	li/món (2 syllables)
horario	schedule	ho/ra/rio (3 syllables)
libro	book	li/bro (2 syllables)
reloj	clock	re/loj (2 syllables)
yoga	yoga	yo/ga (2 syllables)
Quique	Quique (name)	Qui/que (2 syllables)
Igor	Igor (name)	I/gor (2 syllables)
sueño	dream	sue/ño (2 syllables)
albahaca	basil	al/ba/ha/ca (4 syllables)
cooperar	to cooperate	co/o/pe/rar (4 syllables)
período	period	pe/rí/o/do (4 syllables)
búho	owl	bú/ho (2 syllables)
grúa	crane	grú/a (2 syllables)
Uruguay	Uruguay	U/ru/guay (3 syllables)

SINGULAR House Vocabulary

Singular in Spanish	English	Definite article	Indefinite article
casa	house	la	una
puerta	door	la	una
entrada	entrance	la	una
pasillo	hallway	el	un
pared	wall	la	una
ventana	window	la	una
piso	floor	el	un
techo	roof	el	un
luz	light	la	una
dormitorio	bedroom	el	un
habitación	bedroom / room	la	una
cuarto	bedroom / room	el	un
cocina	kitchen	la	una
sala	living room	la	una
comedor	dining room	el	un
baño	bathroom	el	un
terraza	terrace / balcony	la	una
patio	patio	el	un
porche	porch	el	un
sótano	basement	el	un
ático	attic	el	un
garaje	garage	el	un
jardín	garden	el	un
césped	grass / lawn	el	un
flor	flower	la	una

PLURAL House Vocabulary

Plural in Spanish	English	Definite article	Indefinite article
casas	houses	las	unas
puertas	doors	las	unas
entradas	entrances	las	unas
pasillos	hallways	los	unos
paredes	walls	las	unas
ventanas	windows	las	unas
pisos	floors	los	unos
techos	roofs	los	unos
luces	lights	las	unas
dormitorios	bedrooms	los	unos
habitaciones	bedrooms / rooms	las	unas
cuartos	bedrooms / rooms	los	unos
cocinas	kitchens	las	unas
salas	living rooms	las	unas
comedores	dining rooms	los	unos
baños	bathrooms	los	unos
terrazas	terraces / balconies	las	unas
patios	patios	los	unos
porches	porches	los	unos
sótanos	basements	los	unos
áticos	attics	los	unos
garajes	garages	los	unos
jardines	gardens	los	unos
céspedes	lawns	los	unos
flores	flowers	las	unas

Verbs

Pronombres (Pronouns)	hablar (to speak/talk)	aprender (to learn)	escribir (to write)
yo	hablo	aprendo	escribo
tú	hablas	aprendes	escribes
vos	hablás	aprendés	escribís
él / ella / usted	habla	aprende	escribe
nosotros / nosotras	hablamos	aprendemos	escribimos
vosotros / vosotras	habláis	aprendéis	escribís
ellos / ellas / ustedes	hablan	aprenden	escriben

Pronombres (Pronouns)	estudiar (to study)	leer (to read)	recibir (to receive)
yo	estudio	leo	recibo
tú	estudias	lees	recibes
vos	estudiás	leés	recibís
él / ella / usted	estudia	lee	recibe
nosotros / nosotras	estudiamos	leemos	recibimos
vosotros / vosotras	estudiáis	leéis	recibís
ellos / ellas / ustedes	estudian	leen	reciben

Pronombres (Pronouns)	mirar (to look)	comer (to eat)	compartir (to share)
yo	miro	como	comparto
tú	miras	comes	compartes
vos	mirás	comés	compartís
él / ella / usted	mira	come	comparte
nosotros / nosotras	miramos	comemos	compartimos
vosotros / vosotras	miráis	coméis	compartís
ellos / ellas / ustedes	miran	comen	comparten

Pronombres (Pronouns)	enseñar (to teach)	creer (to believe)	persuadir (to persuade)
yo	enseño	creo	persuado
tú	enseñas	crees	persuades
vos	enseñás	creés	persuadís
él / ella / usted	enseña	cree	persuade
nosotros / nosotras	enseñamos	creemos	persuadimos
vosotros / vosotras	enseñáis	creéis	persuadís
ellos / ellas / ustedes	enseñan	creen	persuaden

Adjectives

(Note: The answer key for this section simply provides sample answers that include vocabulary from the book.)

English	Spanish	Feminine Singular	Masculine Singular
big	grande	La taza es grande.	El perro es grande.
small	pequeño / chico	La taza es pequeña.	El perro es chico.
tall	alto	La niña es alta.	El niño es alto.
short (in height)	bajo	La niña es baja.	El niño es bajo.
long	largo	La película es larga.	El lápiz es largo.
short (in length)	corto	La película es corta.	El lápiz es corto.
dark-haired	moreno / morocho	La niña es morena.	El niño es morocho.
blonde	rubio	La niña es rubia.	El niño es rubio.
redheaded	pelirrojo	La niña es pelirroja.	El niño es pelirrojo.
cheap	barato	La película es barata.	El lápiz es barato.
expensive	caro	La impresora es cara.	El auto es caro.
clean	limpio	La casa está limpia.	El auto está limpio.
dirty	sucio	La casa está sucia.	El auto está sucio.
easy	fácil	La tarea es fácil.	El examen es fácil.
difficult	difícil	La tarea es difícil.	El examen es difícil.
close	cercano	La casa es cercana.	El auto es cercano.
far	lejano	La casa es lejana.	El auto es lejano.
full	lleno	La taza está llena.	El auto está lleno.
empty	vacío	La taza está vacía.	El auto está vacío.
happy	feliz	La niña está feliz.	El niño está feliz.
sad	triste	La niña está triste.	El niño está triste.

heavy	pesado	La mochila está pesada.	El libro es pesado.
light	ligero / liviano	La manzana es liviana.	El libro es ligero.
good	bueno	La película es buena.	El libro es bueno.
bad	malo	La película es mala.	El libro es malo.
hot	caliente	La habitacíon está caliente.	El cuarto está caliente.
cold	frío	La habitación está fría.	El cuarto está frío.
new	nuevo	La película es nueva.	El libro es nuevo.
young	joven	Mi hermana es joven.	El hombre es joven.
old	viejo	Mi hermana es vieja.	El hombre es viejo.
antique / ancient	antiguo	La ciudad es antigua.	El auto es antiguo.
poor	pobre	La niña es pobre.	El niño es pobre.
rich	rico	La niña es rica.	El niño es rico.
fat	gordo	La niña es gorda.	El niño es gordo.
thin	flaco / delgado	La niña es flaca.	El niño es delgado.
quick	rápido	La canción es rápida.	El tema es rápido.
slow	lento	La canción es lenta.	El tema es lento.
noisy	ruidoso	La niña está ruidosa.	El niño está ruidoso.
silent	silencioso	La calle está silenciosa.	El camión está silencioso.
safe	seguro	La calle es segura.	El estado es seguro.
dangerous	peligroso	La calle es peligrosa.	El estado es peligroso.
single	soltero	Ella está soltera.	Él está soltero.
married	casado	Ella está casada.	Él está casado.
hard	duro	La mesa es dura.	El libro es duro.

soft / tender	blando	La cama es blanda.	El morral es blando.
soft	suave	La ardilla es suave.	El azahar es suave.
strong	fuerte	La niña es fuerte.	El niño es fuerte.
weak	débil	La niña es débil.	El niño es débil.
dry	seco	La calle está seca.	El baño está seco.
wet	mojado	La calle está mojada.	El baño está mojado.
wide	amplio / ancho	La calle es amplia.	El baño es ancho.
narrow	angosto	La calle es angosta.	El baño es angosto.
delicious	sabroso / delicioso	La manzana está sabrosa.	El café está delicioso.
disgusting	repugnante	La manzana está repugnante.	El café está repugnante.
intelligent	inteligente / listo	La niña es inteligente.	El niño es listo.
wise	sabio	La mujer es sabia.	El hombre es sabio.
silly	tonto	La niña es tonta.	El niño es tonto.
kind	amable	La niña es amable.	El niño es amable.
ready	listo	La niña está lista.	El niño está listo.
cute / pretty	bonito / lindo	La niña es bonita.	El niño es lindo.
ugly	feo	La ardilla es fea.	El rey es feo.
fun	divertido	Una fiesta es divertida.	El tema es divertido.
boring	aburrido	La reunión es aburrida.	El tema es aburrido.
open	abierto	La terraza está abierta.	El techo está abierto.
closed	cerrado	La terraza está cerrada.	El techo está cerrado.
tired	cansado	La niña está cansada.	El niño está cansado.
awake	despierto	La niña está despierta.	El niño está despierto.
crazy	loco	La mujer es loca.	El hombre es loco.

quiet / peaceful	tranquilo	La casa está tranquila.	El techo está tranquilo.
sick	enfermo	La niña está enferma.	El niño está enfermo.
healthy	sano	La niña está sana.	El niño está sano.
sweet	dulce	La manzana es dulce.	El café es dulce.
salty	salado	La carne es salada.	El pez es salado.
fair	justo	La clase es justa.	El examen es justo.
unfair	injusto	La clase es injusta.	El examen es injusto.
careful	cuidadoso	La maestra es cuidadosa.	El chofer es cuidadoso.

Adverbs

English	Spanish	Spanish Adverb
big / enormous	grande	grandemente
tall / high	alto	altamente
long	largo	largamente
clean	limpio	limpiamente
dirty	sucio	suciamente
easy	fácil	fácilmente
difficult	difícil	difícilmente
happy	feliz	felizmente
sad	triste	tristemente
heavy	pesado	pesadamente
light	ligero / liviano	ligeramente / livianamente
cold	frío	fríamente
new	nuevo	nuevamente
antique	antiguo	antiguamente
poor	pobre	pobremente
rich	rico	ricamente
quick	rápido	rápidamente
slow	lento	lentamente

noisy	ruidoso	ruidosamente
silent	silencioso	silenciosamente
safe	seguro	seguramente
dangerous	peligroso	peligrosamente
hard	duro	duramente
soft	suave	suavemente
strong	fuerte	fuertemente
weak	débil	débilmente
dry	seco	secamente
wide	amplio / ancho	ampliamente / anchamente
narrow	angosto	angostamente
delicious	delicioso	deliciosamente
disgusting	repugnante	repugnantemente
intelligent	inteligente	inteligentemente
wise	sabio	sabiamente
silly	tonto	tontamente
kind	amable	amablemente
ugly	feo	feamente
boring	aburrido	aburridamente
open	abierto	abiertamente
tired	cansado	cansadamente
crazy	loco	locamente
quiet / peaceful	tranquilo	tranquilamente
healthy	sano	sanamente
sweet	dulce	dulcemente
fair	justo	justamente
unfair	injusto	injustamente
dangerous	peligroso	peligrosamente
careful	cuidadoso	cuidadosamente